Dear Sandra,

not a fan

daily devotional

Blessings,
Stagecoach Mom

not a fan

daily devotional

75 DAYS TO BECOMING A COMPLETELY
COMMITTED FOLLOWER OF JESUS

kyle idleman

ZONDERVAN

Not a Fan Daily Devotional

Requests for information should be addressed to:
Zondervan, *3900 Sparks Dr. SE, Grand Rapids, Michigan 49546*

Library of Congress Cataloging-in-Publication Data

Idleman, Kyle.
Not a fan daily devotional : 75 days to becoming a completely committed follower of Jesus / Kyle Idleman.
pages cm
ISBN 978-0-310-34409-4 (softcover) – ISBN 978-0-310-34412-4 (ebook)
1. Christian life. 2. Christian life – Churches of Christ authors. I. Title.
BV4501.3.I355 2015
242'.2 – dc23 2015033700

Published in association with Donald W. Gates Jr. C/O The Gates Group, 1403 Walnut Lane, Louisville, KY 40223

Cover photography: TongRo Images / Thinkstock®
Interior design: Kait Lamphere

First Printing December 2015 / Printed in the United States of America
HB 06.09.2020

A special thanks to Brian Sites for all of his help in turning the "Not a Fan" message into a daily devotional. He doesn't just communicate the message, he lives it, and I am thankful for his encouragement and example over the past twenty-five years.

contents

25 days of following

25 days of denying

25 days of pursuing

25 DAYS OF FOLLOWING

The journey really does start here: learning to be a committed *follower*. It could be tempting to jump ahead in a desire to be a spiritual leader. It might sound more productive to prescribe twenty-five days of action steps designed to transform your spiritual life. But it all begins with making a simple decision to follow and learning what it means to live that out daily.

Many Christians and churches work so hard to turn discipleship into a program or curriculum. While those tools can be helpful, the most committed disciples are those who walk closely with their teacher. "What does the Lord require of you? . . . to walk humbly with your God" (Mic. 6:8). Disciples follow well when they know the teacher well.

For these first twenty-five days of our journey together, I simply want to encourage you to deepen your relationship with Jesus. Really get to know him better, again, or maybe for the first time. Even more than that, I pray that knowing him more intimately will lead to following him more passionately. That's why you'll see a daily challenge at the end of each devotion, giving you a practical way to "Follow Today." Wherever you are on your faith journey, I hope you'll take the next step toward

Jesus. None of us has yet arrived. I think you'll find the closer you walk in relationship with him, the more committed a follower you'll become.

DAY 1

the most important question

> Jesus said to his disciples, "Whoever wants to be my disciple must deny themselves and take up their cross and follow me. For whoever wants to save their life will lose it, but whoever loses their life for me will find it."
>
> —*Matthew 16:24–25*

Are you a follower of Jesus?

It's the most important question you will ever answer, and it seems like a good place to begin this journey: Are you a follower of Jesus?

I know. You've been asked this question before. Because it's so familiar there is a tendency to dismiss it. Not because it makes you uncomfortable. Not because it's especially convicting. The question is dismissed mostly because it feels redundant and unnecessary. You recognize that this is an important question for many to consider, but for you? Well, it's like walking into a Boston pub and asking, "Who cheers for the Red Sox?" It's an important question, but you're so sure of your answer, your mind quickly dismisses it. But before you move on too quickly, let me clarify what I am not asking. I am not asking if you go to church or if your parents and grandparents are Christians. I am not asking if you raised your hand at the end of a sermon or repeated a prayer after a preacher. I am not asking if you spent your summers at VBS and/or church camp, have ever worn "witness wear," or understand phrases like "traveling mercies" and "sword drill."

Many of us are quick to say, "Yes, I'm a follower of Jesus," but I'm not sure we really understand what we are saying. One of the most sobering passages in the Bible tells of a day when many who consider themselves to be followers of Jesus will be stunned to find out that he doesn't even recognize them. Jesus describes a day when everyone who has ever lived will stand before God. On that day many who call themselves Christians and identify themselves as followers will stand confidently in front of Jesus only to hear him say, "I never knew you. Away from me." To be clear, that's not my opinion or my interpretation; that is what Jesus has said will happen. Read Matthew 7:21–23.

Whether you've just assumed you are a follower of Jesus or are faithfully walking with him, I pray this devotional journey will encourage you along the way as you reaffirm your commitment to follow him not perfectly but wholeheartedly. And remember we are invited to follow by the grace of God, and it is his grace that will give us the power we need along the way.

following today

Recall that time you first decided to follow Jesus. Where were you? What prompted you to respond? What, if anything, changed about you in those first days and weeks? Write down your answers to these questions: Are you a follower of Jesus? Are you currently living out that decision?

DAY 2

jesus is not a t-ball coach

"Enter through the narrow gate. For wide is the gate and broad is the road that leads to destruction, and many enter through it. But small is the gate and narrow the road that leads to life, and only a few find it."

—*Matthew 7:13–14*

Early on in my preaching and teaching, I tried to talk people into following Jesus by portraying discipleship as appealing, comfortable, and convenient. My intentions were good, but my interpretation was bad.

One of the reasons I wrote the book *Not a Fan* was to consider how Jesus defined what it means to follow him, to be more than just a fan of his. It's also why I keep looking for new ways to encourage people to seek Jesus daily, instead of waiting for someone, even a pastor like me, to spoon-feed them. Most of our praying should involve sitting at Jesus' feet and listening to his strong words with a humble heart and open eyes.

I really hope that when you picked up this book, you weren't looking for a book about Jesus the T-ball coach, who will pat you on the head at the end of each game and tell you not to forget your free snow cone before you go home.

When Jesus described the life of a follower, he described a risky adventure down a narrow and difficult path that only a relatively few will take. The Jesus I know and preach about is unsettling. He is countercultural in an uncool way. And he loves you so much that he tells you the truth even when it is hard to hear. It's *because* he loves you that he talks more about repentance than forgiveness, more about surrender than salvation, more about sacrifice than happiness, and more about death than life. Following Jesus is anything but easy. When we read in the Gospels about Jesus' inviting people to follow him, we see that some people signed up, but many decided to take the easy way out and walk away.

So how about you: Are you ready to follow this Jesus? It is the road less traveled, but it's not a road we walk alone. He is with us every step of the way, giving us exactly the grace and the strength we need as we follow hard after him.

following today

Describe some ways in which it is hard for you to follow Jesus today. Write down a truth, lesson, or teaching of Jesus that is especially difficult for you to act on. How is Jesus specifically challenging you to follow him in a more uncomfortable way?

DAY 3

diy

"I will ask the Father, and he will give you another advocate to help you and be with you forever—the Spirit of truth. The world cannot accept him, because it neither sees him nor knows him. But you know him, for he lives with you and will be in you."

—*John 14:16–17*

In the 1950s, resourceful homeowners began to call themselves do-it-yourselfers. Instead of paying someone to remodel the kitchen or build a new doghouse, they hammered the nails themselves. With good American efficiency, the phrase "do it yourself" soon morphed into "DIY," and these days we have everything from DIY cheesecake baking to DIY music making. Entire television shows are based on the concept of doing it yourself. There's even a DIY Network and a *DIY* magazine. With the help of the internet, people can draft their own legal documents, appraise their own antiques, and even get a DIY divorce.

This do-it-yourself mentality didn't start with enterprising Americans, however. It's really nothing new, going all the way back to the Garden. "You can do it yourself, Eve. You're a smart woman." "You don't need God, Adam.

You can be just like God." And DIY became part of the human DNA.

But Jesus came to change that. God knew we needed a savior, that we couldn't save ourselves. We can't even begin following Jesus by ourselves. Jesus made this clear: "No one can come to me unless the Father who sent me draws them" (John 6:44). And because we need saving help every day, he sent his Spirit to live in the hearts of his people. We were never meant to follow Jesus simply by trying really hard or striving on our own. The Christian journey isn't a DIY project.

Don't buy into the ancient lie. You can't do it yourself. And here's the really good news for Jesus followers: You don't have to.

following today

What's your biggest unsolved problem today, large or small? Describe ways that you have tried to take care of it yourself. Stop to pray a minute. Ask the Holy Spirit (who lives in you) to bring insight and strength.

DAY 4

knowledge versus intimacy

I want to know Christ.

—*Philippians 3:10*

In the Bible, we read about a group of religious leaders known as the Pharisees. The Pharisees knew a lot about God. When someone wanted to play Bible Trivial Pursuit, Godopoly, or Bible Baseball, they were the team to beat. They knew *about* God, but what we discover is they really didn't know him. It's the difference between knowledge and intimacy.

In Matthew 15:8 Jesus describes the Pharisees this way: "These people honor me with their lips, but their hearts are far from me."

That description seems to fit a lot of fans I know. Churches are full of people who go to Bible studies about Jesus, complete with workbooks and homework. Many preachers refer to their sermons as lessons or lectures, accompanied by outlines where church members can take notes and fill in the blanks. I spent a number of years growing up confusing my knowledge about Jesus for intimacy with Jesus. For example, for as long as I can remember I've had the books of the Bible memorized in order—all sixty-six of them. Not only that, but I can actually say the books of the Bible in one breath. Don't try to act like you're not impressed.

Having knowledge is not the problem. But when you have knowledge without intimacy, you're not *really* following Jesus. Like the Pharisees, many people could describe everything they know *about* Jesus. The truth, though, is that Jesus is not impressed by your knowledge or by my talent. What he really desires is our hearts.

following today

Tell Jesus that you want to *know* him, not just know *about* him. Do some honest self-evaluation: Have you spent more time learning about God than learning to fall in love with him? Consider reading through the Gospel of John in the next twenty-one days (just one chapter each day), simply focusing on getting to know Jesus.

DAY 5

the only thing on the menu

Then Jesus declared, "I am the bread of life. Whoever comes to me will never go hungry, and whoever believes in me will never be thirsty."

—John 6:35

Sometimes big moments can cause big problems.

- The actor's mind goes blank at the moment of his big line.
- The singer is forced to mouth "watermelon" as she forgets the words of her song.
- The NBA player air-balls a free throw at a clutch moment.
- The bride can't stop giggling through the entire ceremony. Or crying. Or some really awkward combination of both. (Thankfully, my wife did neither.)
- The preacher calls the groom by the wrong name. (I may or may not have done this. Twice.)

Maybe you've witnessed one of these scenarios. Maybe you've found yourself in one.

I was about to have a big problem at a big moment several years ago. It was Thursday afternoon, and I was struggling to decide what sermon to preach on Easter Sunday. More than thirty thousand people would likely be coming to the weekend services, and the pressure was mounting. Finally, this thought crossed my mind: *I wonder what Jesus taught whenever he had the big crowds. I wonder how he handled the big moments.*

John 6 tells us of one such occasion. With a boy's sack lunch of five loaves of bread and two small fish, Jesus feeds a crowd that likely has grown to more than five thousand. He has never been more popular. After dinner the crowd decides to camp out for the night so they can be with Jesus the next day. But the next morning when the crowd wakes up hungry and looks around for Jesus, aka their meal ticket, he is nowhere to be found. Starving, the crowd is hoping for an encore performance, but Jesus has decided to shut down the all-you-can-eat buffet. In John 6:26 Jesus says to the crowd: "Very truly I tell you, you are looking for me, not because you saw the signs I performed but because you ate the loaves and had your fill."

Then Jesus offers the hungry crowd *himself.* The question is, Would that be enough? Jesus says, "I am the bread of life." Suddenly Jesus is the only thing on the menu. The crowd has to decide if he will satisfy or if they are hungry for something more. Here's what we read at the end of the chapter: "From this time many of his disciples turned back and no longer followed him" (John 6:66).

You see, it wasn't the size of the crowd Jesus cared about; it was their level of commitment.

following today

In your prayers, what do you usually ask Jesus for? Think of a time when he didn't answer your prayer the way you had hoped. How did that affect how you felt about him? Read the rest of this story in John 6. Think of a time when it felt like Jesus was all you had. How did he meet your needs during that time?

DAY 6

the new rabbi

> As Jesus went on from there, he saw a man named Matthew sitting at the tax collector's booth. "Follow me," he told him, and Matthew got up and followed him.
>
> —*Matthew 9:9*

Matthew the tax collector used to be Levi the good Jewish boy. It's likely that he tried to become a disciple of one of the rabbis. Perhaps he was even expected to become a spiritual leader in Israel. But something had definitely gone wrong. Instead of serving the Lord, he decided to serve himself. He turned his back on his own people and became a tax collector for the occupying Roman government. And in those days, there was no such thing as an honest tax collector. They cheated the people to line their own pockets. They were religious and social outcasts, ceremonially unclean, and not even allowed into the outer court of the temple.

Matthew could never imagine that God would still want anything to do with him. Then one day when he was sitting at his tax-collecting booth, a new rabbi came right up to him, extending this simple, life-changing invitation: "Follow me."

Jesus may have been a homeless, unconventional rabbi, but he was a rabbi nonetheless. Rabbis were teachers of

God's Word, and every rabbi had a class of students, or disciples. But this was an exclusive group; not just anyone could be a disciple. Disciples had to earn their way into the rabbi's graces, proving that they possessed an impressive knowledge of Scripture as well as brilliant minds. The rabbi's reputation depended on accepting only the most highly qualified candidates.

But this wasn't the way Rabbi Jesus went about getting followers. Instead of followers applying, Jesus *invited* followers. And in this case, he was inviting the lowest of the low—a tax collector. Someone who was not only a sinner, but who sinned for a living! Someone whose friends were prostitutes, drunkards, and thieves. You know how we know this about Matthew? Because he tells us himself.

These days, people don't know Matthew as a failure and embarrassment who had sold his soul to the Romans for a lucrative job. We know him as a follower of Jesus who wrote the first book of the New Testament.

following today

Have you ever felt disqualified from being accepted by God? How? When did you hear Jesus' invitation for you to follow him? What did you leave in order to respond to that invitation?

DAY 7

simple, but not easy

[Jesus] said to Simon, "Put out into deep water, and let down the nets for a catch." Simon answered, "Master, we've worked hard all night and haven't caught anything. But because you say so, I will let down the nets."

—*Luke 5:4–5*

There's no reason to think that Simon Peter's response to Jesus was sarcastic, but you have to wonder if he was thinking, *Yeah, right. That carpenter-rabbi thinks he can tell a fisherman how to fish?* But what did he have to lose at this point? So as he squinted in the sunlight glinting off the Sea of Galilee, he flung his soaked net overboard one more time.

I'm not sure where those fish had been hiding all night, but this time they swarmed into his net as soon as it hit the water. Simon Peter had never had such a wasted night, and now he had never hauled in a catch like this, in broad daylight. What Jesus suggested wasn't difficult or complicated; it just didn't make any sense. Practically speaking, it seemed like a waste of time. It went against Peter's extensive experience and intuition. Jesus gave no fresh explanation. His directions weren't innovative or creative. Yet Simon Peter simply obeyed.

Sometimes following Jesus is simple, but that doesn't mean it's always easy. Humble obedience to what God has called us to may be as simple as making a phone call, extending an invitation, or walking across the street. Maybe it carries a greater challenge, like extending forgiveness to someone who has hurt you, or moving to a foreign mission field, or trusting him by tithing. But when God asks us to do something that seems impractical or inconvenient—maybe especially when it does—it brings abundant reward.

Notice that God will let you voice your objections. So, if that makes you feel better, he's okay with it. Just remember that the one telling you where to fish is the one who created the fish.

following today

Take a few minutes to read the rest of this story from Luke 5. Prayerfully consider something simple, but not necessarily easy, that Jesus is asking of you today as you follow him. Complete this sentence: "Lord, because you say so, I will . . ."

DAY 8

god stories worth telling

For it is by grace you have been saved, through faith—and this is not from yourselves, it is the gift of God—not by works, so that no one can boast.

—*Ephesians 2:8–9*

As a pastor and a writer, I really get into hearing people's God stories. Often it is my privilege to hear somebody's story firsthand in my office, or in the moments immediately following a weekend service at our church. Many of the stories are the Christian equivalent of rags to riches: Having been thrown out onto the trash heap of life, a person finds Jesus (or rather Jesus finds the person) and everything changes.

These are the kinds of stories that get retold. The details capture our attention: "I remember the day my husband left me, and I was suddenly a single mom with no job." "I cried for days after I got the diagnosis." "Then the stock market crashed and I lost everything."

The outcomes bring glory to God: "My faith community surrounded me in a way my family never had." "I never would have guessed how much God would teach me through the months of chemotherapy and hospital visits." "I learned firsthand that God will supply every need."

Maybe you don't have that kind of dramatic story. The details might seem fairly mundane and ho-hum. You may appreciate it, but other people might not observe much amazing about it. Maybe your story wouldn't make the cut when the book of incredible testimonies is being compiled. But you still have a story worth telling. You have been saved by grace, through faith.

following today

Think about your personal God story. Does it seem revolutionary—or boring? Jot down a chronological outline of it. Try to remember the "mile marker" kind of moments where you put a stake in the ground or turned to go a new direction. Indicate those times when you clearly saw the hand of God at work, providing or guiding.

DAY 9

glory in suffering

> We also glory in our sufferings, because we know that suffering produces perseverance; perseverance, character; and character, hope.
>
> —*Romans 5:3–4*

Most of us don't do suffering very well. We skim right over the word in Scripture, having bought into the false idea that once a person becomes a Christian, everything should be smooth sailing from that point on. We'd prefer to think that suffering is for other people.

It's true that you do see plenty of suffering wherever you go. A simple walk through your neighborhood turns up some: Through an open window, you hear a husband and wife yelling at each other. You find out that your neighbor across the street just got a foreclosure notice. The weedy yard of the elderly couple on the corner tells you that the husband has died and his wife is now in a nursing home. The middle school student constantly on your doorstep has no desire to return to his abusive home.

But when *you* are the one with marital or financial or health problems, suddenly you want to call, "Time out! This isn't how it's supposed to be. I'm on God's team, and he's supposed to make everything right." You run to the nearest marital, financial, or health expert so they can supply you with a quick solution. "Dear God, suffering hurts too much!"

Have you picked up your Bible lately? It's right there in black and white: "In this world you will have trouble" (John 16:33). The point isn't to elude problems and suffering, but to grow and learn from them. As the apostle Paul came to understand, we can actually "glory" in our sufferings, because they produce an abundant harvest—perseverance, character, and hope.

You *are* on God's team, and he *is* making everything right. Remember that this valley you are walking through is only a shadow, and where there is a shadow, there is a light. So keep on walking. Keep following. Because Jesus, too, knows what it means to suffer. And he is walking right beside you.

following today

Read the beautiful and familiar Twenty-Third Psalm. It's only six verses, so read it slowly, more than once, maybe even out loud. As you do, make two distinct lists: In one column, list the verbs that indicate what *you* do (the word *walk* will come up, for example). In a second column, list the things that God does. Thank him for his faithful goodness, comfort, and mercy.

DAY 10

desperate

> Listen to my cry, for I am in desperate need; rescue me from those who pursue me, for they are too strong for me.
>
> —*Psalm 142:6*

Several years ago, when my second daughter, Morgan, was about two years old, I arrived home from my church office early one afternoon. I was eager to spend a little extra time with my young daughter. My wife informed me that Morgan had been sleeping for a while, but gave me the green light to go upstairs and wake her from her nap. I opened the door to her room and quickly noticed two things: First, her dresser had toppled over on the floor and made quite a mess—an obvious, but not necessarily alarming, observation. Second, I noticed that Morgan was not in her bed. Again, easily apparent, but not especially concerning. Until I connected this second fact to the first. In only a few seconds, I realized what had happened. In an attempt to reach something on top of her tall dresser, Morgan had pulled out the lower drawers and started climbing when the entire dresser crashed over on her small body.

I struggled to lift the heavy furniture up as quickly as

possible. Underneath, my daughter was lying still, her body already severely bruised and swollen. I called out for my wife to get in the car, scooped up my unresponsive little girl, and we began speeding to the hospital. My wife sat with our daughter in the back seat and immediately began praying.

While she was praying, I was dialing 911 and there was no answer. To this day, it is the only time I have ever *needed* to dial that number, and the phone simply rang and rang. I hung up and dialed again. Still no response. So I threw the phone in the passenger's seat and joined my wife in her out-loud prayers. Not just any prayers, but passionate, anxious, emotion-filled prayers. Prayers of desperation. Prayers through tears.

The good news is after a number of months Morgan made a full recovery, but I'll never forget the feeling of desperation as I called out to God. Have you ever found yourself in that kind of moment? The time when you had no idea how you would pay the mounting medical bills. The day you came home and found the note from your runaway child. The night your husband stormed out of the house. The appointment where you learned it was cancer. The officer at your door with a bowed head and a tragic report. The silent ultrasound. The joyless marriage. Your first Christmas without her.

Here's what I hope you'll realize: In your moments of greatest desperation, you'll discover that you can depend on Jesus. Desperation fosters dependence. So run to him.

Cry out for him. You'll find a friend who sticks closer than a brother. You'll experience a peace that surpasses your understanding. You'll climb into a strong refuge and a safe hiding place. You'll get to know him as *Immanuel*, "God with you." And you'll learn that he can be depended on when you need him the most.

following today

Read Psalm 88. What words of the psalmist can you identify with? Recall a desperate moment or season in your life. Where did you run for help? Write out several lines of a prayer that begin with this phrase: "I need you to help me with . . ."

DAY 11

when sunday school answers aren't enough

What is more, I consider everything a loss because of the surpassing worth of knowing Christ Jesus my Lord. . . . I want to know Christ.

—*Philippians 3:8, 10*

Several years ago, I listened as a minister friend of mine described a season in his life when he began to question just about everything he had always known about God. My friend had gone through a particularly difficult experience with one of his children, and it proved to be more than just a speed bump in his spiritual journey.

The conversation was more of a monologue than a dialogue. I listened as he vented, and his thought progression was honestly hard to hear. He questioned aloud whether God really worked in all things for good. He struggled believing that a good God would allow something so terrible to happen. He wondered if God wasn't so quick to forgive after all, instead thinking that perhaps God was a vengeful and wrathful God, punishing the child for the past sins of the father. He thought perhaps he had been living a lie all along and doubted he could ever be truly secure in his salvation. And then he summed up his thoughts: "I've heard all those things my whole life; I guess I just got to the point where all the Sunday school answers weren't enough."

I'll be honest. It was one of those moments when I couldn't manufacture a great pastoral response. After all, what right answer could I give him that wouldn't sound trite or rehearsed? What could I tell him that he hadn't heard—and even preached—for years? He had grown up in church. He was a third-generation minister. By this point in his life, he had spent nearly two decades teaching biblical truth to literally thousands of people. But I couldn't help but wonder—maybe his problem was that he grew up knowing the right answers but never really got to know *Jesus*.

The apostle Paul knew all the right answers—he was a well-trained Pharisee and teacher of the law. He had the right lineage, preached the right sermons, and lived the right way. He knew the right people and had the right testimony. But he also had the right perspective: All those right answers and actions proved "worthless when compared with the infinite value of knowing Christ Jesus my Lord" (Phil. 3:8 NLT). And he had the right desire: "I want to know Christ" (Phil. 3:10).

By the way (and this might go without saying), it's not that the Sunday school answers aren't true. It's just that they pale in comparison with knowing the one who said, "I *am* the truth."

following today

Can you identify with this minister's doubts? Think of a time in your own life when you questioned beliefs that you had long held to be true. Is it possible you have spent more time learning the right answers than getting to know Jesus? Pray today that Jesus would reveal himself even more clearly to you as you read his Word.

DAY 12

another wipeout

"You will know that I am the LORD; those who hope in me will not be disappointed."

—*Isaiah 49:23*

Several years ago, I was vacationing with my family at a Tennessee resort. My parents were there, as were both of my sisters and their husbands, as my dad had generously paid the expenses for his three adult children and our spouses to all spend the week together. One sunny afternoon, my two brothers-in-law and I decided to rent bicycles and go for a ride. We picked the bikes up from the clubhouse and set out.

Two important details: (1) At the time, all three of us were in our twenties, so we had plenty of energy to expend. And (2) all three of us are naturally pretty competitive, so we weren't planning a slow, recreational ride.

We were speeding down the first hill—I was in the lead, not that it matters—and preparing to navigate a sharp left turn. I squeezed the handlebar to slow down and suddenly realized what I had somehow failed to notice up to this point: These bikes were not equipped with hand brakes. I had a split-second decision to make: Ride the bike over the curb into the wooded drop-off beyond, or dismount as quickly as possible. (In retrospect, I know I could have used the pedal brake, but this thought didn't occur to me in that moment.) I decided to bail, sending the bike crashing into the trees ahead as I tumbled onto the asphalt below. Even now I can picture the concerned response from my brothers-in-law behind me: clutching their sides, doubled over in laughter, never bothering to ask if I was actually okay.

You've had your share of wipeouts too. You were expecting smooth sailing, but a storm came up. You worked like a maniac to navigate the roadblocks, and you crashed into them instead. You tried to slam on the brakes, but only accelerated into disaster. You were following your dreams, and they turned out to be rabbit trails. Fired from your job. Served with divorce papers. Flunked out of college. Drowning in debt.

Wipeout. Failure. Disappointment. And it's not just situational, but relational too. You reached out for a helping hand only to find pointed fingers. You searched nearby faces for empathy or grace, and instead found ridicule and judgment. Your trust was returned with betrayal, your kindness repaid in abuse.

But God can redeem our failure. He can rescue us when we fall. Those who hope in him will not be disappointed. Those who turn to him find grace and mercy when they need it the most (see Heb. 4:16). When we are humbled, he lifts us up with his strong hand (1 Peter 5:6). And when we fall, he doesn't rebuke, but proves himself mighty to save (Zeph. 3:17).

following today

How were you disappointed most recently? It's not too late to let your personal failure or disappointment point you to God. Write out a prayer—a personal psalm of sorts—expressing your trust in him to turn your defeat into hope. Expect him to come through.

DAY 13

the better thing

"Martha, Martha," the Lord answered, "you are worried and upset about many things, but few things are needed—or indeed only one. Mary has chosen what is better, and it will not be taken away from her."

—*Luke 10:41–42*

Most of us resonate with Martha because we are a distracted culture. We are always on the move, always trying to get something done. Our phones are constantly dinging to let us know there is a text we need to return or an appointment we're going to be late for.

Martha had Jesus right in front of her. I can imagine her grandchildren someday excitedly asking, "What was it like? Jesus in your home! That must have been awesome. What did he say? What was it like to be right there with him?" And Martha would have to respond, "Well, to tell the truth, there were these fancy dishes I was trying to find. I never really even heard what he said. I just caught bits and pieces of the conversation as I flew through the room. Your great-aunt Mary will have to fill you in."

How many times have we been so distracted that we've missed a divine appointment? How often does God long to speak to us, but he keeps getting our voicemail because we're too busy to pick up?

The fruit of busyness seems obvious. Productivity. Effectiveness. Accomplishment. It's easy to equate busyness with virtue or discipline. But Jesus evaluates it through a different lens, and the results become clear. Distraction. Anxiety. Misplaced emotion. So Jesus commended Mary for her choice to quietly sit and listen. To set aside everything there was to *do* and simply take some time to *be with him*. And in the end, Mary chose the best thing; in fact, it was the only thing that was really needed.

following today

Read the rest of this short story from Luke 10:38–42. Think through what dominates your to-do list. What causes you to become "worried and upset"? Are you tempted to view "time away" with the Lord as a distraction from your work? If so, confess your misplaced priorities to Jesus. Then make a conscious choice to sit and listen to him each day. What would happen if, for the next fourteen days, you scheduled time with Jesus at the beginning of each day? Mark it on your calendar. Choose what is better.

DAY 14

jesus is my hero

The Lord will march forth like a mighty hero.

—*Isaiah 42:13 NLT*

Jesus is certainly superhero material. He may not have worn a flashy outfit, complete with leotard and a cape. He might not have had laser vision or bionic legs, but don't let that fool you.

The citizens of first-century Palestine often sought his help. He multiplied a meager lunch into enough food for thousands. With little more than a few words, he transformed jugs of tap water into fine wine. His powerful hands healed incurable illnesses and lifelong disabilities. Violent storms were stilled by the sound of his voice. Demonic minions scattered at the mention of his name. On at least one occasion, he passed through a locked door as if it wasn't even there. And though his sandals must have logged hundreds of miles during his life, he was not limited to such ordinary means of transportation. At the end of his life on earth, he ascended back into heaven without using a helicopter or a rocket suit.

Not even the archenemy Death could defeat him. "Where, O death, is your victory? Where, O death, is your sting? . . .

Thanks be to God! He gives us the victory through our Lord Jesus Christ" (1 Cor. 15:55, 57). Jesus won that epic battle in a most decisive victory, standing up and walking out of his own grave.

Now that's definitely superhero stuff. But do you want to know something truly *incredible*? Something absolutely *amazing*? Something really *awesome*? God gives that same power to those of us who believe in him. It's true. Hard to believe, I know. Not often experienced, I understand. But the better we know Jesus, the more we'll imitate him. And the more we know and follow him, the more we understand the power-filled life that he promises (see Eph. 1:17–23). God wants his power to be a part of your story. He offers you the power to overcome the addiction, release the bitterness, repair the relationship, or whatever else you might add to this list. Nothing is too difficult for the God who conquered death.

following today

Are you living a life of power, or do you regularly feel defeated? In what areas of your life do you feel like you could use some heroic strength? Admit your weakness here. Then pray, believing God's truth for you: "He gives strength to the weary and increases the power of the weak" (Isa. 40:29).

DAY 15

what does your jesus look like?

> The Son is the image of the invisible God, the firstborn over all creation.
>
> —*Colossians 1:15*

As a pastor in a local church, I have many conversations with people who are having a hard time following Jesus. They become entangled again by the same alluring sin. They struggle with maintaining even basic spiritual disciplines. Sometimes they *want* to live for him, and sometimes they *want to want* that. They are exhausted, discouraged, and defeated. They are disappointed in themselves and believe that Jesus is disappointed in them as well.

On occasion, I have asked someone this question: What does your Jesus look like? If you were to draw a picture of him, what would you portray? A few give quick answers, though most have never given it much thought. When they do reply, the pictures are varied and unique. To some, Jesus appears kind and gentle, maybe even a little passive or wimpy. (You've probably seen Jesus' senior picture—you know, the famous one where he's gazing peacefully toward the horizon?) To others, he is an angry and frightening warrior, holding a flaming sword in one hand and a lightning bolt in the other. Sometimes he is smiling, surrounded by children; or assuring—the Good Shepherd caring for his sheep. But one man described his picture this way: "He's standing with his back turned slightly away from me. His arms are folded, and his head is cocked as if to say, 'Really? Come on.' I can't quite see his face, but I don't think he's necessarily scowling or angry. I just think he looks disappointed, wondering why I can't get my act together."

A question struck me as I listened: Who would *want* to follow a Jesus like that? If your image of Jesus has been tainted by your life circumstances, your local church, or your cynical friends, you may not be following the real Jesus. If your picture of Jesus looks more like your disapproving dad or a legalistic preacher or a hypocritical Christian, you might find that following that Jesus just doesn't sound too appealing. And you'd be right.

The good news is, that's not the picture of Jesus the New Testament paints. He is full of truth, yet equally full of grace (John 1:14). He is not condemning (Rom. 8:1), but is instead advocating on our behalf (1 John 2:1). He is a trustworthy guide (Luke 1:79), a friend of sinners (Matt. 11:19), and a watchful shepherd (John 10:11).

And I think you'll find this to be true: As you come to know him as he truly is, you'll be drawn to following him more closely.

following today

What would *your* picture of Jesus look like? Consider drawing him below, if not with a sketch, at least with a description. Does your picture match up with what the Bible teaches about Jesus? Prayerfully begin to repaint his image in your mind today.

DAY 16

jesus is not a registered voter

Again the high priest asked him, "Are you the Messiah, the Son of the Blessed One?"

"I am," said Jesus. "And you will see the Son of Man sitting at the right hand of the Mighty One and coming on the clouds of heaven."

—Mark 14:61–62

Jesus didn't establish any religious organizations. He never identified himself as a capitalist, a socialist, a royalist, a colonist, or any other kind of -ist. He will not define himself in those terms. He's not a Republican, a Democrat, or a member of the Green Party. He does not underwrite liberals or authorize conservatives. Nobody can lay claim to him—not the Catholics, the Protestants, the evangelicals, the charismatics, or the fundamentalists.

Jesus did not incite the Inquisition, endorse the Reformation, sanction the counter-Reformation, validate the Puritans, or divide Ireland. He did not take sides in the Civil War, and he did not write the United States Constitution.

He isn't counting on us to make him famous, and he doesn't need us to help him appear creative, attractive, or really cool. He's not the champion of the hippies because he wore sandals, nor the idol of the hipsters because of his epic beard. Contrary to what your parents might have told you, he didn't wear a suit and tie to church. He probably didn't even go on Sunday mornings. He is not hemmed in by the church's hymns or set free by spontaneity in worship.

You see, nobody can label him; he's the Lord of all. Nothing can confine him; he uses the earth as a footstool. No one can manipulate or control him; he uttered the world into existence with the sound of his voice. Nothing surprises him or catches him off guard. He has never uttered the words, "Hmm, I never thought of that."

He is above all, through all, and in all. He is all-present, all-knowing, and all-powerful. He gives life because he *is* life. He perfectly loves because he *is* perfect love. He alone is God. And we stand in awe of him.

following today

Take several minutes today to stand in awe of Jesus. Pick one or two great worship songs (allow me to recommend "Clear the Stage" by Jimmy Needham, and "Name Above All Names" by Awaken Worship, both available for download on iTunes) to listen to. Heed the advice of the psalmist: "Be still, and know that I am God" (Ps. 46:10). Then pray this prayer from Habakkuk 3:2: "Lord, I have heard of your fame; I stand in awe of your deeds, Lord. Repeat them in our day; in our time make them known."

DAY 17

he calls us

> In love [God] predestined us for adoption to sonship through Jesus Christ, in accordance with his pleasure and will—to the praise of his glorious grace, which he has freely given us in the One he loves. In him we have redemption through his blood, the forgiveness of sins, in accordance with the riches of God's grace that he lavished on us.
>
> —*Ephesians 1:4–8*

The highest view, in my thinking, of God's sovereignty is not that God causes everything; it's that he causes everything to work together for his good purposes (see Rom. 8:28). That's a whole other level of sovereignty and power—he takes whatever happens and, in his all-encompassing wisdom and power, uses it to accomplish his work and his purpose.

Let me try to illustrate this. Suppose that I, as a wise and loving father, knew that my son was going to be an all-star football player when he grew up. (By the way, when my son was three years old, my wife asked him, "So what do you want to be when you grow up?" He did, in fact, answer, "A football player!" But then he threw something else in there that he had never before mentioned. He said, "When I grow up, I want to be a mermaid." *What?!* I finally said, "That's merman, buddy, merman.") If I had this certain knowledge, wouldn't it significantly change most everything about the way I raised him? I wouldn't bother spending much money on piano lessons or art class. Those glazed doughnuts? Not in my house. Video games would be replaced with exercise regimens. Monday Night Football would take precedent over *America's Funniest Home Videos.* I would use my newfound knowledge to guide my son to his certain destiny.

In much the same way, God knows our ultimate destiny. He already sees our truest identity. And so his purpose is to draw us closer to Jesus. He uses everything that happens—even the bad stuff—to do this. Whether it's our own fault or someone else's, God has predestined everything to work together to pull us along toward him, and to shape us in the process. He doesn't waste anything. We can follow him with confident faith, trusting that he is already working things out for our good and his glory.

following today

Think back over significant events of your life. Can you trace God's hand bringing you to where you are today? What circumstance in your life right now is *beyond* your ability to understand? Write it down and profess your trust in our good, sovereign God. (To consider a little further: What would you change today if you knew your ultimate destiny? Here's a little secret: you do.)

DAY 18

no exception clause

"Lord, the God of Israel, there is no God like you in heaven above or on earth below—you who keep your covenant of love with your servants who continue wholeheartedly in your way."

—1 Kings 8:23

I saw a report on MSNBC about a group of new vegetarians. They interviewed one of the new vegetarians, a twenty-eight-year-old woman. One of her quotes captures the viewpoint of the group: "I usually eat vegetarian. But I really like sausage." She represents a growing number of people who eat vegetarian but make some exceptions. They don't eat meat, unless they really like it. As you might imagine, the real vegetarians aren't real happy about the new vegetarians. They put pressure on the new group to change their name. And so here's the name they chose for themselves: flexetarians. As I watched the report, I realized something; I'm a flexetarian. I absolutely refuse to eat meat, unless it's being served. The young woman on MSNBC explained it this way: "I really like vegetarian food, but I'm just not 100 percent committed."

A lot of people follow Jesus this way. They compartmentalize the areas of their lives they don't want him to have access to. They try to negotiate the terms of the deal: "I'll follow Jesus, but I'm not going to sell my possessions. Don't ask me to forgive the people who hurt me; they don't deserve that. Don't ask me to save sex for marriage; I can't help my desires. Don't ask me to give a percentage of my money; I worked hard for that cash. I really like Jesus, but I'm just not 100 percent committed." They call themselves Christians. They follow Jesus, but they've made some exceptions.

But following Jesus requires a complete and total commitment. Jesus never left open the option of *selective* commitment. He allows no exception clauses. You don't get to say, "I will follow Jesus—except in this area of my life, where I will do things my way." You can't treat the call of Christ like a spiritual all-you-can-eat buffet, picking and choosing as you go through the line. There is no such thing as a flexetarian when it comes to faith. If you call yourself a Christian, by definition you are committing yourself to follow Jesus in every area of your life.

following today

Honestly evaluate your commitment to Christ. Do any areas of your life come to mind where you have withheld complete commitment? Have you inserted an exception clause that shouldn't be there? What will you do about it?

DAY 19

getting to know you

"Lord, Lord," they said, "open the door for us!"
But he replied, "Truly I tell you, I don't know you."
—*Matthew 25:11–12*

When I take my wife out to eat on a date, she won't let me face the TV in the restaurant. She knows I get distracted watching whatever is on. It could be sports or it could be a special on knitting, I still get sucked in. And I don't really see the problem with it. If there is a lull in the conversation and we don't have anything to talk about, what's the harm in watching a little TV?

I never really understood why this was an issue until one night when we went out to eat and I got distracted watching two couples at different tables. At one table was a young couple clearly in love. They may have been newlyweds, but my guess is they were still dating. They were sitting on the same side of the booth, snuggled up, talking nonstop, laughing at each other's jokes. Their food was getting cold, but they didn't care. At the table next to them was an elderly couple, and I'm guessing they had been married for decades. They didn't say a word. Nothing. I watched as they just sat there in silence. I finally pointed this out to my wife, saying,

"Look at that. Isn't it kind of sad? It starts off one way, with this young couple just talking, talking, talking, and then decades later, you have this older couple just sitting there in silence. It's sad." And my wife said, "I think it's kind of sweet."

At first I was confused by her reply. Until it hit me: It was sweet because they didn't *have* to say anything. Being together, focused on each other, even in silence, was a picture of the kind of relationship my wife wants. She doesn't care about the nice dinner. She isn't impressed by my expensive gifts, kind words, or thoughtful acts. She wants my heart. She wants to know me.

Ultimately, that's how our relationship with Jesus will be defined. Our acts of piety, our adherence to religion, our observance of rules and rituals—none of this will impress him. More than he wants our words of affection, our tithe dollars, or our acts of service, he simply wants to know us and for us to know him.

following today

How well do you know Jesus? Write down a list of things you already know about him. Consider looking up his "I am" statements (the good shepherd, gentle and humble in heart, the way, the truth, the life, etc.) in the Gospels using an online search engine.

DAY 20

listen carefully

"Therefore consider carefully how you listen. Whoever has will be given more; whoever does not have, even what they think they have will be taken from them."

—*Luke 8:18*

A friend of mine told me about a woman in our church who had recently begun following Jesus. This woman had lived most of her life outside of church and, quite frankly, just didn't have much interest in spiritual things. But then she met my friend, an authentic Christ follower, at her local gym and was drawn to what she saw. The woman began attending church regularly, soaking up everything she was learning. Her spiritual growth was dramatic and quick. In fact, it seemed so rapid that it alarmed my friend, who confided in me, "I'm just afraid that the seed isn't growing deep enough roots."

My friend was referring, of course, to a familiar parable that Jesus told about good and bad soil and how they receive the seed of the Word of God. And Jesus himself gives this challenge: "Therefore consider carefully how you listen" (Luke 8:18). He knew it to be true: Some people hear the Word, but before they can do anything, the devil, like an opportunistic roadside crow, snatches it away from them. Others receive the Word, but it cannot take root because of their rock-hard hearts. Still others (and this was my friend's concern) hear and receive the Word, but before it can come to maturity in their hearts, the thorny cares of life choke it to death.

But some who hear the Word have hearts that are ready, like good soil with good growing conditions. They not only hear and receive the Word of God but nurture its growth and allow it to bear mature fruit in their lives. These are the ones who have and will be given more, while the other listeners will lose the farm. How you hear is what's so critical.

By the way, when the seed fell on the "good soil" in Jesus' story, it "yielded a crop, a hundred times more than was sown" (Luke 8:8). As it turns out, my friend's friend was "good soil." So, as you might expect, her roots are already growing deep. And it wouldn't surprise you to know that the seed is yielding an even greater crop. Her son was baptized just five months later; her husband decided to follow Jesus within the same year.

As you follow Jesus, "consider carefully how you listen" to his Word. Seize it; retain it. Persevere in it, then get ready for an abundant harvest.

following today

Read this entire parable (Luke 8:1–15). Describe the soil of your heart. Is it ready to receive—and to bring to maturity—the Word of the living God? Are you harboring any worries that might "choke out" God's Word in your life?

DAY 21

fanatics for jesus

Zeal for your house consumes me.

—Psalm 69:9

"Everything in moderation." Sounds like a prudent way to live, doesn't it? Seems like reasonable advice for a happy, balanced life.

But it just doesn't fit when you're talking about following Jesus. Jesus doesn't say, "Everything in moderation." He isn't interested in enthusiastic admirers who don't get too carried away. He wants completely committed followers.

I met a young man a few years ago whose life radically changed when he started following Christ. Instead of (in his words) "going out, drinking, smoking pot, and chasing girls," he was constantly at church, serving however he could. He quit working during church hours, even though, as a single dad, he needed the hours. He started giving generously even though finances were tight. He wouldn't be quiet about what he was learning from the sermons and even started talking about going on a mission trip. After just a few minutes with him, anyone could easily see the joy that he had found in Christ.

Some time after his radical change, his mom wanted to

meet with me. I thought for sure I knew what she wanted to talk about. I knew that she went to a different church, and I assumed she wanted to express her appreciation to me and to our church for the positive changes in her son's life. But that wasn't the case. She was upset with him. She blamed me and our church, saying, "My son has taken all of this too far."

But you see, when it comes to following Jesus, there is no middle ground. Moderation isn't an option. You can't walk a fine line or sit on the fence. Jesus says if you don't sell out completely, you can't be his follower. His invitation is an all-or-nothing one. How will you answer his invitation today?

following today

Take time to do some honest self-assessment. Consider what those closest to you would observe in your life when it comes to the following areas:

- **Serving.** Am I joyfully contributing to the work of the ministry, or do I sit back and let others serve?
- **Giving.** Am I bringing my whole heart—talents, time, and resources—to the church, or do I give only when I have some extra?
- **Meeting with believers.** Do I make it a priority to be in God's house each week, or do I attend every now and then?

- Bible study and prayer. Do I meet regularly with the Lord, or is my time with him only haphazard and occasional?

Think about this question: Would anyone accuse me of following Jesus too zealously?

DAY 22

rest your soul

> "Come to me, all you who are weary and burdened, and I will give you rest. Take my yoke upon you and learn from me, for I am gentle and humble in heart, and you will find rest for your souls. For my yoke is easy and my burden is light."
>
> —*Matthew 11:28–30*

Most of the concerns that weigh you down were not given to you by God. Family problems, unemployment, toxic workplaces, chronic illness, and worries of all kinds—these burdens may seem to come with your role as a parent, a student, a breadwinner, or a caretaker. Some of them you may have picked up yourself, trying to make your life "just right."

But when Jesus invites us to share his yoke, somehow the burden gets lighter. His burden doesn't weigh us down. Jesus said so: "My burden is light."

When Jesus said, "Come to me, *all* you who are weary and burdened," he meant everyone. Those of you whose cargo has been there so long you've forgotten the lightness of traveling without it. Those of you who don't know another way to live. All who are tired of shouldering the load can come to him.

The yoke is easy now, because the weight has shifted. The burdens that used to seem crushing are bundled up with his. The concerns we could hardly bear seem manageable. They are part of our calling as a parent, student, provider, or caretaker. We find that we can do "everything through Christ, who gives [us] strength" (Phil. 4:13 NLT). I love how *The Message* paraphrases Jesus' invitation: "Keep company with me and you'll learn to live freely and lightly" (Matt. 11:30 MSG). Being yoked with him is the best way of trusting and praying.

following today

Our burdens come in all shapes and sizes and durations, and I wouldn't be surprised if you feel weighed down by something right now. Try this: Hold your hands out, palms facing upward. Now picture your burden resting in your hands. Lift your burden to him as you pray, asking him to help you live freely as you follow along with him.

DAY 23

"it is finished!"

When he had received the drink, Jesus said, "It is finished." With that, he bowed his head and gave up his spirit.

—John 19:30

The last word that Jesus spoke on the cross was the word *tetelestai*, which is translated "It is finished." In the Greek-speaking world of the time, the term was written on official documents to indicate that a bill had been paid in full, kind of like a rubber stamp that says PAID. Therefore, when they heard *tetelestai*, the people at the foot of the cross (and those who read John's account afterward) would have made the unmistakable connection: The death of Jesus Christ had paid in full for their sins.

When we read "It is finished," we don't automatically get that full meaning. We hear it in a sort of flat, unemotional way. To us it kind of sounds like "Game over," like what the head coach might say to the assistant coach as the seconds wind down in a losing game. "It's finished; we're done." But that's not how Jesus uttered it. He was finished, all right—finished winning.

See, the term was also used in the Greek-speaking world

as a cry of victory. People would shout it in the streets as a conquering army returned home: "*Tetelestai!* The battle is over! Victory is ours! Celebrate!"

We follow a victorious King, yet many followers of Jesus still drift along in the doldrums of defeat. We languish in loss. We walk with bowed heads and slumped shoulders—frustrated in our battle against sin and perplexed about our next move.

But on the cross Jesus Christ won the victory in the battle of the ages. On the cross, he was making two decisive statements: He had paid in full the entire sin debt of all humankind, and he was declaring victory for us as well. "We are more than conquerors through him who loved us" (Rom. 8:37).

following today

What sin struggle is threatening to defeat you? Are you walking in discouragement and failure, or could you dare to believe that sin has already been defeated? Write out a "victor's prayer" over your battles. Don't write it as if victory hasn't yet been achieved; claim a decisive victory today. *Tetelestai!*

DAY 24

pay attention to those signs

"Enter through the narrow gate. For wide is the gate and broad is the road that leads to destruction, and many enter through it. But small is the gate and narrow the road that leads to life, and only a few find it."

—*Matthew 7:13–14*

Some time ago I was returning to Louisville from a quick trip to Cincinnati. The highway between Cincinnati and Louisville is called I-71. It's a straight shot, and the trip takes about an hour. I was heading home in plenty of time to have dinner with my family. I had the radio turned up, it was a beautiful day, and I was enjoying the journey. After about an hour I knew I was getting close to Louisville, but then I saw a sign that said "Welcome to Lexington."

I had made the frequent mistake that others had told me about. Right outside Cincinnati is a place where, if you're not really careful, you can easily miss where I-71 toward Louisville splits off from I-75 toward Lexington. For close to an hour I was completely convinced I was on I-71, but all along I was on I-75. It never occurred to me that I might be going the wrong way. With the radio blaring, I was singing along to the music, completely oblivious. I never allowed for the possibility that I was on the wrong road.

Jesus noted a similar problem regarding two roads in life. One is easily traveled by many people. The other is easily missed—only a few will find it. But many of those on the crowded highway still think they're moving in the right direction. "Many will say to me on that day, 'Lord, Lord, did we not prophesy in your name and in your name drive out demons and in your name perform many miracles?' Then I will tell them plainly, 'I never knew you. Away from me, you evildoers!'" (Matt. 7:22–23).

Those are sobering words. They were busy *doing* the right things, but their accomplishments didn't make them true followers. They never *knew* Jesus, and he didn't know them. Fortunately for you and me, there's still time to regain our bearings.

following today

Some questions for your journey: Does your life reflect what you say you believe? Do you think you're on the right road because of what you've done? Do you know Jesus, and does he know you? I don't expect you to have quick, ready answers to these questions. But it would do you some good to "pull over" and meditate on them today.

DAY 25

better than gps

> Lord, I know that people's lives are not their own;
> it is not for them to direct their steps.
>
> —*Jeremiah 10:23*

I have a GPS on my phone, but I rarely use it. I usually tend to think I know where I'm going, even when I don't. For the most part, every time I do use the GPS, it's because I've already tried finding something myself but have managed to get lost. When I finally type the destination into my phone, the first question that comes on the screen is this: "Directions from current location?" In other words, "Do you want to start where you are?"

The answer to that question seems obvious enough, right? Of course I want to start from here. I'm not even sure where "here" is, but I'm confident that I want to start from here. And as soon as I answer that question affirmatively, the GPS begins calculating my route—not from where I started before I lost my way, not from the direction I should be headed or from a point farther along my journey, but from right where I'm currently located.

So why does such an obvious answer *physically* seem to elude people *spiritually*? I've discovered that the most common reason people give for not following Jesus is that they want to get their lives together first. They want to get a few things squared away or take care of some personal issues. They want to start their journey from somewhere else than where they are currently located.

When Jesus invites you to follow him, he wants you to start right now from your current location. You don't have to go back to where you started. You don't need to get a little closer on your own. He reaches out to you with grace and love and invites you to follow him. Feeling weak? Depend on his strength. Trapped in sin? Find freedom in his endless mercy. Been down this road before? Know that he is still patiently waiting for you to come home. Lost? Trust his directions. Jesus wants you to start following him from right where you are—and he wants you to start right now. It promises to be an incredible journey.

following today

Describe your current spiritual location. Far from home? Lost off-road somewhere? Closer than you've ever been? Write out a prayer committing to follow Jesus wherever he leads. Affirm your desire to follow him, right now, from right here.

a follower's prayer

God, I want to be a follower of your Son, Jesus. I am learning that following Jesus just means growing closer to him and becoming more like him. The problem with following Jesus is that I know me, and I am not like him. His character, love, and rightness don't match the real me. I need your help to follow. I can't do it on my own. I ask for your grace and strength to give me everything I need to be more like Jesus. On this journey of understanding what following Jesus means, open my eyes to see that following is more about who you are than who I am. I want to know you. Just as you know me—better even than I know myself!—I want to really know you.

Today I am surrendering my willpower to be a better me and instead allowing you to be at work in me, making me more like you. Thank you for helping me follow you. Thank you for leading me to this book where my desire to follow you more closely is fed. I can't be a follower without your Holy Spirit showing me how to do it. My longing to be a follower of Jesus is as real as my weakness. So I give you my heart, mind, and body in order to follow. Thank you that you not only lead me but also show me how to follow. I am ready. Lead on.

Amen.

25 DAYS OF DENYING

You can't follow after Jesus without denying yourself. Jesus puts it quite simply: "Whoever wants to be my disciple must *deny themselves*" (Luke 9:23, emphasis added).

To deny yourself isn't just the idea of saying no to yourself—or even resisting yourself. It's not simply giving up something you really, really want. It's so much more than putting something off for the delayed gratification of receiving it at a later date. The idea of denying yourself is that you don't look in your own direction. It's saying, "I choose Jesus. I choose Jesus over my family. I choose Jesus over career goals. I am his completely. I choose Jesus over getting drunk. I choose Jesus over looking at porn. I choose Jesus over a redecorated house. I choose Jesus over my freedom. I choose Jesus over what other people may think of me."

A follower makes a decision every day to deny self and choose Jesus, even if it costs everything.

DAY 1

pull the plug

> Jesus said . . . "I am the resurrection and the life. The one who believes in me will live, even though they die; and whoever lives by believing in me will never die." . . .
>
> Jesus called in a loud voice, "Lazarus, come out!" The dead man came out, his hands and feet wrapped with strips of linen, and a cloth around his face.
>
> —*John 11:25–26, 43–44*

Lazarus did not have a near-death experience. Even Miracle Max from *The Princess Bride* would have realized that he was not simply "only mostly dead." He was completely, undeniably dead. First, he was miserably sick, and then he passed away. He expired. He kicked the bucket. He bought the farm. He bit the dust. However you want to say it, make no mistake about it: Lazarus died. His sisters washed his body and wrapped it in linen. Weeping, they laid his corpse in a cave-tomb and leaned a flat stone across the opening.

We like to read this story because it ends so well, with Jesus arriving apparently too late—four days later—only to dramatically raise Lazarus from the dead and give him back to his family.

I wonder, though, if we devote enough time to thinking

about the implications for our own lives. In our excitement about the resurrection part, do we forget that you can't raise a person from the dead unless he or she is actually *dead*? Do we really get it—that we need to be dead people ourselves before Jesus can infuse us with his life?

Second Corinthians 5:17 says, "Therefore, if anyone is in Christ, the new creation has come: The old has gone, the new is here!" Colossians 3:3 says it even more clearly: "For you died, and your life is now hidden with Christ in God." The expectation is obvious: When Jesus invites us to follow him, it's an invitation to die. Only when we die to ourselves can we truly live for him. That kind of surrender goes against every instinct we have. We want to hang on. We can't seem to let go. We refuse to pull the plug. But it is only when we die to ourselves that we can finally experience the resurrection power of Christ.

denying today

Someone said that the hardest part of dying to ourselves is that we have to do it *daily*. Write out a prayer for today, laying your life at the feet of Jesus. Reaffirm that he is not just your Savior, but your Lord. Don't hurry through this, and prayerfully write only what you mean. For *today*, list what attitudes, priorities, or sins—what part of *you*—you will allow to die.

DAY 2

too many gods

"You shall have no other gods before me.

"You shall not make for yourself an image."

—*Exodus 20:3–4*

Idolatry isn't just one of many sins; rather it's the one great sin that all others come from. It's not *an* issue; it is *the* issue. There may be a hundred million different symptoms, but the issue is always idolatry. If you start scratching at whatever struggle you're dealing with, eventually you'll find that underneath it is a false god. And until that god is dethroned, you will not have victory.

God isn't interested in competing against others or being first among many. He will not be part of any hierarchy. God declines to sit atop an organizational flowchart. He *is* the organization. He is not interested in being president of the board. He *is* the board. He is God, and your life will not work until everyone else sitting around the table in the boardroom of your heart has been fired. There can be no partial gods, no honorary gods, no interim gods, no assistants to the regional gods.

God designed and created the universe to work this way, and he's the sole owner and operator of it. So only the one true God knows how it works. He is the only God who can help us, direct us, satisfy us, save us.

By the time we read Exodus 20, we see that God has had it with imitation and substitute gods. He tells Israel to break up the pantheon ("many gods"). All other god activity is canceled. He makes sure the people understand that he is the one and only. He is the Lord God.

You may be thinking this is not a problem today. But my guess is that our list of gods is longer than ever. We may not have the god of commerce, the god of agriculture, the god of sex, or the god of the hunt. But we do have portfolios, automobiles, adult entertainment, and sports. Simply calling them by different names doesn't change who they are.

When someone or something, good or bad, replaces the Lord God in the position of glory in your life, then it has by definition become a god.

denying today

Just this week, what drew your attention the most? What does your checkbook or calendar or to-do list reveal about your priorities? What people or things keep sneaking into your mind and blocking your view of God? Be honest here; see if you can't identify by name some of the gods who have set up thrones in your life.

DAY 3

not a good trade

> The people made a calf at Mount Sinai; they bowed before an image made of gold. They traded their glorious God for a statue of a grass-eating bull.
>
> —*Psalm 106:19–20 NLT*

While God was giving Moses the Ten Commandments on Mount Sinai, the people waiting below whined because it was taking so long. Moses had left his brother, Aaron, in charge, and the people clamored for a god to lead them—a god they could see, touch, and worship. So they gathered everyone's gold, melted it down in the fire, and made a golden calf to worship. A little bit ironic, don't you think? At the very moment God was telling Moses about having no other gods before him, the people down below were crafting their own custom god.

It seems pretty plain to see: That's not a good trade. They exchanged the Creator God for a god of their own creation. But are we really any different? We replace God with statues of our own creation—a house we constantly upgrade, a promotion that comes with a corner office, a team that wins the championship, a body that is toned and fit. We work hard at creating our own golden calves.

Maybe you're thinking this is a stretch. After all, you could take any pursuit, goal, or achievement—anything that anyone was ever devoted to!—and make it out to be idolatry. And you'd be exactly right. Anything at all can become an idol once it becomes a substitute for God in our lives. Let me say it another way: Anything that becomes the purpose or driving force of your life probably points back to idolatry of some kind.

But it's never a good trade. Why trade knowing the Prince of Peace for a substance that provides temporary escape? Can possessions and riches that rust and run out ever compare to eternal riches that will never fade? Could what your mother or father or a professor or friend or employer thinks of you ever matter more than the affirmation of the One who knows you best and loves you most?

Exodus 32 records what happened when Moses came down from the mountain. Moses was mad, and God was even angrier. Moses had the golden calf ground down to powder, sprinkled it in the people's water supply, and then made them drink it. And they learned the hard way that what they believed would satisfy actually, in the end, had a bitter taste.

denying today

Make a list of as many attributes of God as you can think of (for example, his love, power, peace that passes understanding, provision). Now look over the list and do some honest self-evaluation: What have you "created" to put in the place of any of those things in your life? (Some examples: affirmation from others, providing for yourself, success and achievement.) Confess your own golden calves.

DAY 4

disordered loves

"People are slaves to whatever has mastered them."

—2 Peter 2:19

When Momma's not happy, ain't nobody happy." It's kind of a funny old saying, but you know it's true. Regardless of whether you're a momma yourself, I'll bet you have firsthand experience of the power of an unhappy momma over the mood of the rest of her family. And the opposite is also true. Sometimes the reason Momma's not happy is because she has allowed other family members to dictate her frame of mind. Everyone—moms and dads and kids—can give up too much control to others, allowing somebody or something besides God to steer their emotions up or down.

Who's first? God or your troubled teenager? Who's in charge? The Prince of Peace or your two-year-old tantrum thrower? Do your family members' issues and outbursts command too much of your attention? Of course we are to love our families. But if a family member consistently has control of our mindset and our emotions, it may be an indicator that God is being replaced. Jesus tells us, "If anyone comes to me and does not hate father and mother, wife and children, brothers and sisters—yes, even their own life—such a person cannot be my disciple" (Luke 14:26). In Jewish culture, *hate* was used to express "a lesser form of love." What Jesus is saying is that our love for God should far eclipse our love for our families.

The early Christian leader Augustine coined the term "disordered loves." He was talking about legitimate objects of love that have fallen out of order, much like a misbuttoned shirt. Loving and honoring your parents is a good thing, even one of God's top ten commands. Loving your wife or husband is a really good thing, even a way that we imitate the heart of Jesus. But the centrality and sheer magnitude of our love for God, expressed as worship, can only be applied in one direction. God won't share the throne of your heart with your spouse, your children, or your friends. But he will not commandeer your "disordered loves." Instead, like the perfect Father he is, he will wait patiently for you to return to your first and best love.

Then and only then will you be free to love others well. Or let me say it this way: We love others best when we love God most.

denying today

What person or people matter most to you in this world? Is there a relationship in your life that seems to be the determining factor in whether you are happy and joyful or sad and depressed? Can you find disordered loves in your family relationships? Repent for your misplaced relationship priorities and ask the Lord to help you shift your top priority back to him.

DAY 5

the real problem is . . .

Let us examine our ways and test them, and let us return to the LORD.

—Lamentations 3:40

Recently I ran into our local Walmart to buy some ink for our printer. I don't understand why the ink costs more than the printer, but that's not my point. Anyway, as I was heading down the aisle, I saw some shorts for sale. Summer was just around the corner, I could use a pair of shorts, and they cost all of ten bucks. So I grabbed a pair of size 34 shorts off the rack and put them in my basket. The next day, I put on my new shorts and immediately realized they were a little tight. I mean, I could get them buttoned, but that poor button was hanging on for dear life.

Do you know my first thoughts as to why the shorts didn't fit? Well, here's what I *didn't* think. I didn't think, *Huh, I must have put on a few pounds over the winter.* I didn't think, *I guess I haven't really been watching what I eat.* I never even considered for a moment that the shorts were too tight because something was wrong with *me.* Instead, I thought, *Well, I guess you get what you pay for. Walmart must have mismeasured these shorts.*

Here's my point: Pointing our finger in the wrong direction will keep us from addressing the actual issue. The ability to deny ourselves begins with an honest assessment of where any problems lie. After all, why would you want (or even need) to surrender or sacrifice if everything in your life was already in order? Why would you need to make a life change if you aren't the one at fault? Who would expect you to admit a wrongdoing if someone else is to blame? Denying ourselves means realizing the truth that "there is no one righteous, not even one" (Rom. 3:10). It requires acknowledging that we are not excluded from the "all [who] have sinned and fall short of the glory of God" (Rom. 3:23). It demands praying this risky prayer of King David: "Search me, God, and know my heart" (Ps. 139:23).

Denying myself starts with looking in life's dressing room mirror and admitting that the problem is not with the shorts.

denying today

Read 1 Corinthians 6:9–11. Have you ever been "deceived" in some area of your life, denying that the problem is with you? Pray out loud this short prayer from Psalm 139: "Search me, God, and know my heart; test me and know my anxious thoughts. See if there is any offensive way in me, and lead me in the way everlasting" (vv. 23–24). Now *listen.* Have ears to hear. What truth about you is God revealing? Don't sugarcoat it or mince words. Write it down, and surrender it today to him.

DAY 6

smell you later

> Who will rescue me from this body that is subject to death? Thanks be to God, who delivers me through Jesus Christ our Lord!
>
> —*Romans 7:24–25*

Do you ever find yourself struggling with things that you thought you had left behind a long time ago? When I was in high school, I remember being on my way to pick up a girl for a date. As you might expect, I had to walk through her front yard. As you might not expect, it was a minefield of doggie-doo. And being nervous about the date, of course, I wasn't watching where my big feet landed.

Her mom answered the door, smiled politely, and invited me in. As I sat on the sofa next to my date, I noticed a certain unpleasant aroma. I had no clue about its source. I sniffed my date, which, in retrospect, wasn't a good move for a new relationship. I leaned toward her parents—it wasn't them either. The source of the smell was me. I was ground zero! I looked down at my Doc Martens and realized that I had really stepped in it this time. Not only that, but I had tracked it through the entryway, across the carpet, and into the family room. Suddenly I wasn't breathing well.

Some of us have mistakenly believed that once we became Christians, life would be free of complications, smooth sailing, a rosy journey with no splinters or thorns along the way. No trials or difficulties. No sins, no struggles. *No doggie-doo*. But even the apostle Paul discovered that following Jesus simply doesn't work that way: "Although I want to do good, evil is right there with me" (Rom. 7:21). He described a sin nature that just kept on waging war, even making him a prisoner. Paul concluded with this self-evaluation: "What a wretched man I am!" (v. 24).

It's hard to understand, because we know our sins are forgiven, but we still have the old desires, the old habits. And this is the challenge for many of us. The problem is that we have tried to follow Jesus without leaving something behind.

denying today

What are the habits, desires, and sins that still cling to you? What *stuff* in your life should have been destroyed a long time ago but is still managing to come along for the ride? Maybe you'd be honest enough to write them down, with today's date, and surrender them anew to the lordship of Jesus. Memorize Romans 7:25.

DAY 7

where is your cross?

> He called the crowd to him along with his disciples and said: "Whoever wants to be my disciple must deny themselves and take up their cross and follow me."
>
> —*Mark 8:34*

A Christian father was getting ready to give his Christian daughter in marriage to an atheist, and he was rightly concerned about it. So he asked me, as a pastor, to meet with the young man. A pastor having lunch with an atheist sounds like the beginning of a joke, but he and I hit it off immediately and talked for hours. After he told me his story, I presented the gospel to him. It was the first time he had heard most of what I shared. At the end of our conversation, we prayed together, and he repented of his sins and confessed that he believed Jesus is the Son of God. I was amazed that God crossed our paths at just the right time.

The young couple got married and the husband's new faith and commitment grew rapidly. One day after about a year, he called me. He had been married for eight months and told me that things were going well. But he went on to explain that his father-in-law was upset with him, and he wanted to ask me what he should do. His father-in-law felt that his son-in-law should "throttle back" his faith. Apparently, he had been taking God's Word seriously in the area of tithing, and his father-in-law felt the money would be better used saving up for a house. The older man also disapproved of his son-in-law's decision not to work on Sunday so he could worship God in church. The father-in-law said, "I'm really glad you've become a Christian, but Jesus never wanted you to become a fanatic."

In other words, "I'm glad you're following Jesus, but why don't you put your cross down?"

Jesus, though, makes it clear that a decision to follow him is a decision to die to yourself. He didn't come to this earth to modify your behavior or tweak your personality or fine-tune your manners or smooth out your rough spots. Jesus didn't even come to earth to change you, making you a new and improved version of yourself. The truth of the gospel is that Jesus came so that you would die to your old way of life—and then live a new life for him. He came so that you would be like him. If you want to be his disciple, you *must* take up your cross daily and follow him.

denying today

In what ways is your story like the young man's above? In what ways can you resonate with the father-in-law? What does your cross look like? In other words, describe areas of your life that you have sacrificed (or that you need to sacrifice) in order to fully follow Jesus. Meditate on this for a few minutes: If someone who knew you before you became a Christian were to describe how you've changed, what would they say? Would they accuse you of becoming a fanatic?

DAY 8

humbled to be exalted

"Do not do what they do, for they do not practice what they preach. . . . Everything they do is done for people to see. . . . Woe to you, teachers of the law and Pharisees, you hypocrites! . . . Woe to you, blind guides! . . . You snakes! You brood of vipers!"

—Matthew 23:3, 5, 13, 16, 33

Matthew 23 records one of Jesus' last sermons here on earth. It's a sermon traditionally known as "The Seven Woes," and it is directed at the religious leaders of the day—the Pharisees. In this particular sermon, Jesus holds nothing back. If you grew up thinking of Jesus as a Mr. Rogers character who was always smiling, winking at people, and wearing a sweater vest, the tone Jesus takes with these religious leaders may surprise you. He isn't trying to *fix* the Pharisees; he's not simply giving them a warning or a caution. Jesus isn't offering them counsel or advice. He is strongly opposing these religious leaders because he doesn't want people to confuse following the rules with following him.

The word *woe* is both an expression of grief and a curse, and Jesus repeats it multiple times. He is saying to the Pharisees, "Cursed are you. You're afflicted and tormented."

And he is saying to us, "Don't imitate these leaders." Jesus is not impressed with their fancy robes, wordy prayers, or self-righteous authority. He takes issue with the way they operate. And Jesus doesn't want his followers to imitate them or admire them.

Instead, he wants us to "imitate God" (Eph. 5:1 NLT). He calls us to deny ourselves and have the "same mindset as Christ Jesus" (Phil. 2:5). He practiced what he preached: "For even the Son of Man did not come to be served, but to serve, and to give his life as a ransom for many" (Mark 10:45). He reminds us that in his kingdom, "anyone who wants to be first must be the very last, and the servant of all" (Mark 9:35). And he used the Pharisees to illustrate this "upside-down way of Jesus" truth: "For those who exalt themselves will be humbled, and those who humble themselves will be exalted" (Matt. 23:12).

denying today

Read Philippians 2:1–11. Write down several words or phrases that jump out at you. Take a quick but thorough inventory of your last several days. Describe a time when you demonstrated "selfish ambition or vain conceit." Is there someone you need to make amends with because you didn't consider or value them above yourself? When did you look out only for your own interests? Humbly confess these things to the Lord. Then picture the greatest servant of all—Jesus—humbly washing your feet, forgiving your sin, extending his grace.

DAY 9

finding nemo

> I said to myself, "Come now, I will test you with pleasure to find out what is good." But that also proved to be meaningless.
>
> —*Ecclesiastes 2:1*

When we lived in California, our oldest daughter was four and she wanted a pet. I agreed, but there were a few conditions. The pet had to be something that didn't bark, meow, or make any kind of noise. It couldn't shed any kind of fur or hair. And the pet had to cost less than five bucks. Within those limitations, we finally settled on a goldfish.

At the store, the fish tank featured a sign offering a "three-day guarantee, no questions asked." To me, this seemed like a safe policy and even good stewardship, not an omen.

Back home, my daughter named him—or her, who knows?—Nemo. She wanted to play with her new pet, but how do you play with a fish? You can't take it for a walk or teach it to fetch. But you *can* take it swimming. So we took a trip to the swimming pool. I explained to my daughter that the chemicals in the pool would not be good for a fish, so we brought Nemo in a glass cup filled with water and set the cup on the very edge of the pool. While my daughter and I were splashing in the water, I noticed that Nemo was watching us. I figured he wanted to get out of the cup and into the vast ocean that the swimming pool must have looked like to him.

After a few minutes I looked over again to check on Nemo, but the cup was empty. Apparently the lure of freedom on the high seas was so strong that Nemo had flip-flopped out of the cup and into the pool. I tried to catch him, but catching a goldfish in a swimming pool is more difficult than you might think. Eventually Nemo rose to the surface, belly up. My daughter wasn't too upset when I reminded her of the three-day guarantee.

Nemo might have been having the time of his life, but what he didn't know was that what promised pleasure was really bringing poison. When pleasure becomes our primary pursuit, it delivers the opposite of what it promises. Pleasure has this unique trait: The more intensely you chase it, the less likely you are to catch it. Philosophers call this the "hedonistic paradox." The idea is that pleasure, pursued for its own sake, evaporates before our very eyes.

Jesus painted this sharp contrast: "The thief comes only to steal and kill and destroy; I have come that they may have life, and have it to the full" (John 10:10). Here is the powerful truth I hope you discover: When we worship God by denying ourselves, we experience what we were really wanting all along—deep and ultimate pleasure.

denying today

Think for a moment about the pain that pursuing pleasure has brought you. Write down a time (or times) when the pursuit simply didn't deliver what it had promised. We are told to count the cost of following Jesus, but for a few minutes, consider the cost of pursuing pleasure instead.

DAY 10

money, more money

> "No one can serve two masters. Either you will hate the one and love the other, or you will be devoted to the one and despise the other. You cannot serve both God and money."
>
> —*Matthew 6:24*

You knew we'd get to this issue at some point, right? The god of money has been around a long time. Oh, you used to know him as gold or silver, heads of cattle or animal skins—pretty much anything that could be traded. These days he goes by cash, dough, bacon, benjamins, moolah, bank, and the list goes on. He might even take the form of a plastic card or be a file named "portfolio."

Money has grown so dominant in our culture that it's difficult for us to stand far enough back to get a perspective. No matter what we may say, many of us live as if the pursuit of wealth is the real goal in life. Sometimes we hear rich people say things like "Money doesn't make you happy," but most of us think they all probably flew first class to some exotic destination where they got together and agreed to say that to make the rest of us feel better.

We pay lip service to the idea that money isn't very

important, but the way we spend our time and the things we pursue reveal our true beliefs. For many, the ultimate fantasy is winning the lottery or inheriting a fortune from some rich relative.

The wisest—and wealthiest!—man who ever lived, King Solomon, recognized that "whoever loves money never has enough; whoever loves wealth is never satisfied with their income" (Eccl. 5:10). The apostle Paul, who knew what it was like to live both with wealth and in poverty, came to this conclusion: "My God will meet all your needs according to the riches of his glory in Christ Jesus" (Phil. 4:19). It might surprise you to know that even Jesus spoke a great deal about money. Of the thirty-eight parables he told that are recorded in the Gospels, sixteen deal with the topic of money.

And he spelled out a pretty succinct bottom line: You cannot serve both God and money.

denying today

Have you fallen into the trap of serving the money god? Test yourself with these revealing questions: How often do you compare what you have and how much you make to others? How much anxiety do finances add to your life? To what extent are your dreams and goals driven by money (or the lack of it)? What is your attitude toward giving? Maybe today you would consider giving some money away even before someone asks.

DAY 11

no happier now

Watch out! Be on your guard against all kinds of greed; life does not consist in an abundance of possessions.

—Luke 12:15

My wife and I were young, newly married, and living in a tiny house that cost $25,000. The monthly payment is etched into my memory, as numbers tend to be when you don't have much: $213 per month. That seven-hundred-square-foot home was the best we could manage, and we looked on the bright side. For example, you just had to plug in the vacuum cleaner once—its cord could reach every wall in the house from one outlet. And we certainly didn't get tired running up flights of stairs or jogging over to "the west wing." It was small, but it was cozy.

We didn't have central heat, for that matter; we had a floor furnace that took up most of the only hallway in the house. There wasn't room on the sides to walk around it, and it was too long to step over. So to avoid burning your feet in the winter, you had to take a running leap to clear it. The house did not have double-paned windows, so ice formed on the *inside* of our windows. It was my job to get the ice scraper from our car and scrape the ice off the windows inside the house. The walls were paper thin, so if the dog next door was barking, or his stomach was growling, we heard it in high fidelity. I'm fairly certain that the one bathroom we had was taken out of a small airplane.

We were full-time college students, and we were technically living well below the poverty line. We ate Ramen noodles three nights a week. A night on the town meant ice water for two and then splitting an appetizer. Our goal was to keep the check under six bucks. Yep, the servers loved us.

Years later, my wife and I were lying in bed reminiscing and playing "Can you top this?" with austerity stories, cracking each other up. Then we grew quiet and she said, "Are you any happier now than you were then?" I didn't even have to think. "No," I said. "I'm not."

That story isn't unique; if you've been alive for a while, you can probably tell a similar one. Even though we know experientially that money won't satisfy us, still we always seem to be chasing it. But the Bible reminds us many times that our lives are not measured by how much we have and that wealth can never really satisfy. So Paul gives this advice to young Timothy: "Flee from pursuing wealth; don't put your hope in money. It is so uncertain. Be rich in good deeds. Be satisfied with having food and clothing. 'Godliness with contentment is great gain'" (see 1 Tim. 6:6–19). It's advice worth heeding.

denying today

Sit with your spouse or a close friend and tell some of your own "remember when" stories. Ask yourselves the same question: Are you any happier now than you were then? Read 1 Timothy 6:6–19, and then write several phrases of Paul's advice regarding money and possessions. Underline the ones you most need to be reminded of today.

DAY 12

merit badges

So we fix our eyes not on what is seen, but on what is unseen, since what is seen is temporary, but what is unseen is eternal.

—2 Corinthians 4:18

Personal achievement is a very powerful and alluring idol.

Think about our experience as children. Cub Scouts to Boy Scouts; Brownies to Girl Scouts. These are wonderful organizations that teach many positive values—in particular, the value of achievement. Learn to tie a knot; you win a merit badge. Go on a hike and fulfill the given requirements, and you earn that colorful "camping" patch. If you were a member of a scouting group, do you remember how great it felt when the scoutmaster or den mother pinned that patch to your uniform?

Or maybe as a high school athlete you got the letter jacket for your sport, and every year you worked hard to add pins and patches to your jacket to show your achievements. Maybe it was the "1" rating at the state music competition or the blue ribbon watermelon you entered at the state fair or the stack of perfect attendance certificates or academic scholarship awards—the list goes on and on. Many kids find their identity and value in what they achieve. They put their hope in what they *one day* might be able to achieve.

So the vest plastered with badges, the jacket covered in patches, the trophies weighing down the shelf, the ribbons and pins and medals, the report cards, the diplomas and degrees, the promotions, raises, and bonuses can all become idols to which we bow. For some, it simply translates to a daily checklist completed, a spotless kitchen, or a perfectly manicured lawn. These are all tangible representations of what we have achieved through hard work and dedication.

I'm not saying there's anything wrong with any of these achievements. In fact, they can be acts of worship that glorify God. But when our lives are all about getting things accomplished, we discover there's not much room left for God. Our approach to worshiping God may be like checking off a box on our to-do list labeled "go to church" or "read the Bible."

Denying ourselves means not placing so much focus and energy on these temporary, tangible trophies. Instead, we look beyond to what is unseen, to what has eternal significance: "achieving . . . an eternal glory that far outweighs them all" (2 Cor. 4:17).

denying today

Go ahead, brag on yourself just for a minute: What awards or achievements are you most particularly proud of? Whose congratulating voice do you most appreciate hearing? Think through what you're currently working hard to achieve. Hard work is good, but honestly evaluate: Why are you doing it? To prove yourself? To compete against someone? To provide a comfortable life? Pray these words from the apostle Paul: "But whatever were gains to me I now consider loss for the sake of Christ. What is more, I consider everything a loss because of the surpassing worth of knowing Christ Jesus my Lord, for whose sake I have lost all things. I consider them garbage, that I may gain Christ" (Phil. 3:7–8).

DAY 13

success upside down

> Jesus looked at him and loved him. . . . "Go, sell everything you have and give to the poor, and you will have treasure in heaven. Then come, follow me."
>
> At this the man's face fell. He went away sad, because he had great wealth.
>
> —*Mark 10:21–22*

We don't even know his name. This rich young ruler was probably well known to the people of his time, but we have no clue what became of him. Chances are, he went on to become the richer, older ruler, playing the game of life pretty well.

His conversation with Jesus began with what seemed like a great question: "What must I do to gain eternal life?" The problem was that the rich young ruler was used to getting things done. On his own, by himself. When he wanted to get something done, he had the means, the energy, and the authority to make it happen. And we get the sense that when he asked Jesus that important question, he was ready to check another thing off his bucket list and collect another lifetime achievement award.

But Jesus redefines a successful life as one that humbly says to God, "I can't do this on my own. I need your help." Jesus takes success and turns it upside down. So he challenges the young man head-on. Give up your self-sufficiency. Stop depending on your own resources and abilities. Depend entirely on me.

If only he had answered Jesus differently. Then I imagine we'd know his name. Maybe there would have been thirteen disciples instead of twelve. Maybe there would have been five gospels instead of four.

Instead, "he went away sad, because he had great wealth." Doesn't that sound ridiculous? He went away sad *because* he was rich? People don't go away sad because they're rich; they go away sad because they drive a seventeen-year-old three-cylinder Kia. Why would having so much make him sad?

Because he had too much to give up. He owned so much that it owned him. He was a rich young ruler, and Jesus was offering him an opportunity to be a poor young servant. But the god of success took his hand and led him away.

Humility is a consistent theme with Jesus. It was the first thing he addressed in his Sermon on the Mount: "Blessed are the poor in spirit, for theirs is the kingdom of heaven" (Matt. 5:3). "Poor in spirit" isn't a reference to the size of your checking account or retirement portfolio. These words describe people who know they don't have it all figured out, people who are humble enough to ask for help.

The rich young ruler was one right answer away from treasures he could not even imagine, but he backed away, unwilling to heed the very advice he had asked for.

denying today

Write down your definition of success. What would have to happen for you to be successful? Remind yourself that God measures success by faithfulness, by obedience. Read Matthew 25:21, then write your own commendation from Jesus. Prayerfully consider: What will he praise you for?

DAY 14

power down to power up

> Truly my soul finds rest in God; my salvation comes from him.
>
> —*Psalm 62:1*

I'll never forget the first time I went to a church service in Haiti. I had heard from other friends who had gone on similar mission trips about worship services lasting four to six hours. Most people walked to get there, and once they arrived, they would stand crowded together in un-air-conditioned buildings. No coffee, tea, or doughnuts after the service, either.

I was impressed with that level of commitment. Most preachers here in the States would tell you that they start losing people if the church service goes much longer than an hour. There's also the pressure of making sure that hour is filled with enough song and dance and multimedia to captivate the congregation. Can you imagine the members of your church leaving home an hour early in order to walk to the church, staying there for half the day, and then trudging back home under the hot afternoon sun? It seems pretty far-fetched.

So when I got to Haiti, I spoke to the local Haitian pastor

about the time differences in our services. I asked, "What is it about the Haitian people that keeps them worshiping at church for so many hours?" It really was a mystery to me, and I was hoping for a profound answer that would redefine my ecclesiology.

He laughed and replied, "In Haiti, we have nothing else to do."

I laughed with him, but then I was almost immediately struck by the weight of his answer. They didn't have televisions, radios, smartphones, laptops, tablets, or movie theaters. The Lord God didn't have much competition. And then I realized the implications of that truth.

The psalmist observed that God leads us beside quiet waters (Ps. 23:2). The prophet Jeremiah knew that it is good to wait quietly for the Lord (Lam. 3:26). Jesus invites us to get away with him to a quiet place where we'll find rest (Mark 6:31). God himself says it this way: "Be still, and know that I am God" (Ps. 46:10).

What if you eliminate God's competition, just for a test, and see what happens? Turn off the TV. Log off Facebook. Turn down the music. Unplug the game console. And turn your eyes to the Lord.

denying today

What kinds of media and entertainment captivate you the most? Is there any device you just "couldn't do without"? Well, try it. Take the challenge. "Go Haitian" for the next seven days. Consider a "media fast," other than your work requirements. Turn your full attention to the most fascinating Presence of all. He is more than enough.

DAY 15

be still

> Be still, and know that I am God; I will be exalted among the nations, I will be exalted in the earth.
>
> *—Psalm 46:10*

I read about an interesting social experiment that was conducted in 2007 by a writer at the *Washington Post.* At a Metro subway station in Washington, DC, on a cold January morning, a man with a violin played six Bach pieces for about forty-five minutes. He was casually dressed and wearing a baseball cap. Hundreds of people passed by while he played, hurrying on their way to work or other obligations.

After several minutes, a three-year-old boy stopped to listen, but his mother impatiently tugged him along. Several other children did the same thing, but every parent—without exception—forced their children quickly along. One woman threw a dollar in his open violin case but never stopped to listen. In all, about twenty people gave money—about thirty-two dollars in all—but kept on walking at their normal pace.

During forty-five minutes of continuous playing, only six people stopped and listened for a short while. Interviewed later, most people would say they didn't even notice that someone had been playing a violin. When he finished, no one noticed or applauded. There was no recognition at all.

Here's the irony: The violinist was Joshua Bell, one of the greatest musicians in the world. Just two nights before, he had played in a sold-out Boston theater where concertgoers paid an average of one hundred dollars a seat to listen as he played the very same music. In the subway, passersby threw their loose change into the case of his violin, an instrument worth 3.5 million dollars.

How often do you hurry through life without taking time to notice the beauty of life around you? From the moment your alarm rouses you each morning to the instant your tired head hits the pillow at night, the day is full of *noise*—cell phones, talk radio, hurried conversations, instant messages, popular music, television, social media. All with the potential to crowd out the "still, small voice" that whispers to us: *Come away to a quiet place. He who has ears to hear, let him hear. Be still, and in your stillness, you will come to know that I am God.*

denying today

For some of us, busyness props up our own self-importance. When is the last time you just sat still, in silence? Try it now. For just five minutes, be still. (I think it was the Karate Kid's mentor who wisely said, "Being still and doing nothing are two very different things.") This week, turn off the radio. Silence your phone. Shut down your machines for a chunk of time each evening. Give yourself the gift of stillness.

DAY 16

take captive

> Though we live in the world, we do not wage war as the world does. . . . We take captive every thought to make it obedient to Christ.
>
> *—2 Corinthians 10:3, 5*

The Bible says that our thoughts determine who or what we worship. Proverbs 4:23 instructs, "Above all else, guard your heart, for everything you do flows from it." Let me reword that for you: Be careful how you think, because what you think about determines what you will worship. That's why the Bible tells us to take every thought captive.

Psychologists have given us increasing insight as to how that happens. The field of cognitive psychology examines how our thoughts shape our attitudes, emotions, and behavior. They're all intertwined, but our mind is the all-important starting point.

Experts say that the first time you think a new thought, it's like blazing a trail through the woods. In your brain, this new thought carves what is called a "neural pathway." Like the wooded trail, at first the path is barely visible. But then the trail begins to get used, and before long, it becomes a well-trodden path that looks as if it's been there forever.

Children and teenagers are especially busy carving out the trails of their young thought processes. Adults build plenty of new pathways too. I read a study about a young man who viewed pornography on his computer, with a baseball cap on top of the computer's screen. After some time elapsed, it was shown that he could be sexually aroused by the sight of a baseball cap. He had worn a mental path that he will find nearly impossible to change. Remember, this is mental warfare.

So we choose to go to war. We decide to take prisoners. We take captive every thought that meanders down the road and subject it to Christ's command. Taking every thought captive means we wrestle every thought to the ground and force it to submit to Christ. One way or another, there will be a prisoner. Either we take our thoughts captive by the power of the truth, or we'll find ourselves taken captive and imprisoned by lies.

denying today

What thought pathways are you reinforcing in your mind? Where will they lead you? Philippians 4:8 gives us a great filter for our thought life. Read it and memorize it. Ask God to make you more conscious of what is on your mind.

DAY 17

a slave of jesus

> Simon Peter, a servant and apostle of Jesus Christ, to those who through the righteousness of our God and Savior Jesus Christ have received a faith as precious as ours: Grace and peace be yours in abundance through the knowledge of God and of Jesus our Lord.
>
> *—2 Peter 1:1–2*

When Peter began writing his second letter, he didn't introduce himself by saying, "Peter, a best friend of Jesus, present at the Mount of Transfiguration, featured preacher on the day of Pentecost." Instead, he simply wrote, "Simon Peter, a servant"—or, translated more accurately, "a slave." John, Timothy, and Jude all give themselves the same title. James didn't begin his letter by saying, "James, the half brother of the Son of God." He began by saying, "James, a slave of God and of the Lord Jesus Christ" (James 1:1 NLT). When Paul wrote to the church in Rome, he began by identifying himself as "a slave of Christ Jesus" (Rom. 1:1 NLT).

Most of us grew up in homes where we were taught to study hard in school so we could get a good job and make lots of money and live in a big house, drive a nice car, and enjoy great vacations. When you ask a child what they want to be when they grow up, the answer generally reflects that influence. No kid ever says, "When I grow up, I want to be a slave." In fact, most of us would find the idea of slavery offensive because of what occurred in past history. But that is what the Bible calls us to. The Bible teaches that the highest calling for you and for me is to be a slave to Jesus.

Sure, there are other ways we identify with Christ. He is a friend of sinners, a master teacher, and the head of his church. He is the promised Messiah, a conquering King, and the omnipotent God. We are lost sheep, and he is the Good Shepherd; we are sinners, and he is our Savior. But when we call Jesus "Lord," we aren't saying any of those things. We are saying, "He's the master, and I am the slave."

In fact, we can't call Jesus "Lord" without declaring that we are his slaves. The two terms are inseparable. As crazy as it might seem to everyone else, as ridiculous as it might appear to those who don't understand, we *choose* this life of slavery. Nobody will ever be forced into slavery to Jesus. Out of love, we willingly submit to his lordship.

When we fully surrender all that we have and all that we are to him, we discover the strangest thing: It's only by becoming a slave to Jesus that we can truly find freedom.

denying today

Write down the words "slave" and "master." What words and ideas come to mind for each of those roles? What are the slave's responsibilities to the master? What are the master's responsibilities to the slave? As you pray today, submit yourself again as a slave of Jesus, and thank him for being a perfect, loving master.

DAY 18

snuggie theology

"Whoever wants to save their life will lose it, but whoever loses their life for me and for the gospel will save it."

—*Mark 8:35*

We are by nature comfort seekers, not cross bearers. We are the people of the La-Z-Boy, the country club, the day spa, and the Snuggie. Have you seen this product advertised? It's a blanket with sleeves. At first I thought it was a ridiculous idea. But the more I saw the Snuggie, the more I wanted one. So when my wife asked me what I wanted for Valentine's Day, I was surprised by the words that came out of my mouth: "I want a Snuggie." That's a phrase you never plan on saying as a grown man. I was excited about a blanket with sleeves. When it arrived, I put it on and thought, *Wait a second, I already have one of these. This is just a bathrobe that you put on backwards.*

Unfortunately, many churches have developed what I call Snuggie Theology. They try to make sure everyone is as comfortable as possible. They promise health and wealth to all who follow Jesus. They promise you a luxury car and a beautiful home. But contrast the image of the Snuggie with the image of the cross. One represents ease, the other symbolizes pain. One promises comfort, the other calls for sacrifice.

Yet people buy into this Snuggie Theology—until their finances run out, their family falls apart, or their health takes a turn for the worse. That's when they start to question God, suspecting that he isn't holding up his end of the deal. When they expected to put on a comfortable Snuggie, they are not going to be happy when they are told to take up a cross.

For the Christ follower, the slogan is "Die Daily," and the symbol is the cross. The point is the ultimate surrender of yourself—your dreams, your accomplishments, your comfort. You see, when you're dead, you're no longer concerned with your life—instead, you are free to live for Christ.

denying today

What are the implications of dying daily for you personally? Can you think of anything (or anyone) you've *lost* for the sake of following Christ? When have you denied yourself in a way that actually made you uncomfortable?

DAY 19

dead elephant in the room

> I do not understand what I do. For what I want to do I do not do, but what I hate I do. . . . As it is, it is no longer I myself who do it, but it is sin living in me.
>
> —*Romans 7:15, 17*

Jesus slaughtered sin on the cross. But sin's dead carcass still occupies a lot of living space, and it stinks to high heaven. Like the elephant in the room that no one wants to talk about, it exercises a powerful influence over everything. It is a powerful rival to righteousness.

I resonate with Paul's lament in Romans 7. Just when I think I have gained victory over some sinful response, I get a powerful whiff of death again. Reeling and gagging, I too often find myself doing the very thing I said I wouldn't do. And I hate it.

Hating it is a good start, because God hates it too. His Holy Spirit is called "holy" (set apart, consecrated to God) for a reason. And he always stands ready to help me get back on my feet for another round. We may be down, but we are not out. God has promised us all the help we need to achieve victory over sin. If we ask his Spirit, he will disarm the beast within us. He will drain the life out of our sinful habits, one by one.

Many people get frustrated in their efforts to follow Jesus. They're trying as hard as they can to "get it right," and they don't understand why they are having such a hard time. They determine again to be faithful, and hate themselves for being so inconsistent. One young man sent me an email that read, "Thanks so much for this challenge to go from fan to follower. I am trying every day to become a follower of Jesus." I appreciated that, but I can tell you he is going to fail because "trying every day" simply isn't enough. Changing just one word in that email would make all the difference in the world. It needs to read, "Thanks so much for this challenge to go from fan to follower. I am dying every day to become a follower of Jesus."

denying today

Read Romans 7:15–25. In what areas of your life can you identify with Paul? What good do you want to do, but don't? What sin do you want to distance yourself from, but can't? Write them down, if you dare. Then surrender your list to God in prayer, thanking him for rescuing and delivering you through Jesus Christ our Lord (Rom. 7:25).

DAY 20

king of the hill

The Philistine commanders continued to go out to battle, and as often as they did, David met with more success than the rest of Saul's officers, and his name became well known.

—*1 Samuel 18:30*

When I was in fourth grade, we played a game called King of the Hill every day at recess. It's a pretty simple concept, really: All the boys would push and shove each other to the ground, and when the whistle blew, whoever was left standing on the hill was crowned king. My guess is that most schools have outlawed such games these days because of the sheer brutality. But I loved this game. You know why? Because as a fourth grader I was the same size as I am now and already shaving. I was the undisputed, undefeated king of the hill.

I was enjoying my reign as king until the day a new student joined our class who was bigger and taller than I was. Worst of all, this student was a girl. And not just *any* girl. She wore cowboy boots. She made fun of the girls in our class who wore braids. She ate glue. And sure enough, at recess that day, she wanted to play King of the Hill. She dug her boots in the ground and came after me. And when the whistle blew that day, I had been dethroned by a girl; I was no longer king.

I've discovered that King of the Hill isn't just a childhood game we play. It often becomes our life's pursuit: Do whatever it takes to make it to the top, and stay there. The appeal of success seems obvious. It's about position and authority, prestige and clout. It's about having the right seat at the table, the right space in the parking lot, the right title on the business card. It's about getting the crown, the trophy, the promotion, or the award. Success is finding out how the score is kept, and then scoring.

The word *success* is rarely used in the Scriptures, but one of the closest biblical equivalents is the word *blessed*. Even today, we tend to use that word as the humbler way of saying, "I'm successful." A guest comes by and says, "You have a beautiful home. I love your sports cars and your yacht." And you smile modestly and say, "I've been blessed."

But think about the difference between those two words. *Success* is the word we use to speak of something we have accomplished ourselves. *Blessed* indicates not that you have done something, but that something has been done for you. Let me put it this way: Success is when we achieve; blessed is when we receive. If we say, "I'm successful," we are giving the glory to ourselves. When we say, "I'm blessed," we are giving the glory to God.

denying today

True success is hearing Jesus say to you one day, "Well done, good and faithful servant!" (Matt. 25:21, 23). How will he measure your success? Read Jesus' statements of *blessing* from his Sermon on the Mount in Matthew 5:1–12. Can you resonate with any of those whom Jesus calls "blessed" (the poor in spirit, those who mourn, etc.)? Set a timer for just three minutes. Write down as many blessings as you can think of in that time. Then pray, thanking God for the blessings he has lavished on you.

DAY 21

soul food

Whether you eat or drink or whatever you do, do it all for the glory of God.

—1 Corinthians 10:31

Eating is good. (Did I just hear an "amen"?) Yet every gift God gives us can be twisted into a lure to pull us away from him.

The gods of food work overtime in the United States. You walk into a restaurant, an environment filled with stimulating sights and smells. The host hands you a menu so thick it has to be divided into chapters, illustrated with mouthwatering photographs. Nobody goes into such a place simply for bodily sustenance. It's all about *satisfaction*, isn't it? We are looking for a little slice of heaven. In fact, we seem to invoke heaven or spirituality quite often where food is concerned: "This cake is heavenly," "This pie is out of this world," "soul food," "angel food cake," "nectar of the gods."

Food can be just as much a god for people who would never eat anything except organic health foods. Some people build their lives around diet and exercise, obsessed with outward appearance and enticed to worship their own image.

Whether you eat to indulge or eat to be healthy, either

way you can be drawn into serving something other than the God who created the food itself. In the Scriptures, food is always a gift from heaven. God himself showed Adam and Eve the great bounty of good things he had prepared for them to eat. He designed us to *enjoy* eating, not simply to eat as a matter of sustenance. He created a vast spectrum of foods and flavors. He even tells us, "Go, eat your food with gladness" (Eccl. 9:7).

But we'll never be fully satisfied until we find our satisfaction in him. Jesus calls himself "the bread of life" (John 6:35). And when we come to him, we'll never go hungry; when we believe in him, we won't thirst again. Even though we can't see it, *he* is the food we're really looking for.

denying today

Next time you sit down for a meal, say grace with fresh appreciation for what God has provided. Deny food power over you; it can't assuage your guilt, and it won't provide any lasting comfort. Instead, acknowledge that God himself has provided everything we'll ever need—physically and spiritually—and be grateful.

DAY 22

slow down and fast

> "When you fast, do not look somber as the hypocrites do, for they disfigure their faces to show others they are fasting. Truly I tell you, they have received their reward in full. But when you fast, put oil on your head and wash your face, so that it will not be obvious to others that you are fasting, but only to your Father, who is unseen; and your Father, who sees what is done in secret, will reward you."
>
> —*Matthew 6:16–18*

I grew up going to potluck dinners. If the term *potluck* is unfamiliar to you, think of it as the "white elephant gift exchange" concept applied to churchwide fellowship dinners. It's a meal where each family brings something to eat and sets it out on the table for everyone to share. You never know what you're going to get. A lot of it is not that desirable, like the Jell-O salad that consists of leftovers such as beets, tuna fish, Spam, Velveeta cheese, and peanut butter mixed together with Jell-O. Or the marinated carrots my grandmother always brought. I begged my mom to take something good, like a bucket of fried chicken or her Oreo ice cream dessert. I remember many church events that centered around these meals. But I can't remember a single one that celebrated fasting.

To fast is to voluntarily abstain from food for spiritual purposes. But fasting has been neglected in the church for a long time. When was the last time you heard a sermon about it? (Could the church be fasting from fasting? I don't think that counts.) It is mentioned in the Bible as many as seventy-seven times, and although God does not command us to fast, Jesus seems to assume that we will. (Notice that he says "when," not "if.")

Fasting is not the same as a crash diet. Its goal isn't a "quick cleanse" or rapid weight loss. It is not meant to make us appear more spiritual to others or look better in the sight of God. Instead, it is an expression of grief over loss or sorrow for sin. Fasting displays mastery over our bodies and tangibly demonstrates our dependence on God. For millennia, God's people have fasted to empower their prayers or to ensure safety. In the New Testament, believers fasted to seek God's guidance. Jesus himself fasted forty days and nights in the wilderness before setting out on his public ministry.

Fasting simply brings us closer to him. By denying ourselves what our bodies often crave the most, we dedicate our entire worship in love to the God who sustains us.

denying today

Privately declare a fast—not in order to fit into your skinny jeans or swimsuit, or even as a test of your discipline. Fast for the express purpose of spending time with God. Choose a water-only fast for one day or three days, or fast from specific foods for the next week or two. Pray that you will have a greater hunger for God and his Word than for the food of this world.

DAY 23

whining or worshiping?

> Do everything without grumbling or arguing, so that you may become blameless and pure, "children of God without fault in a warped and crooked generation."
>
> —*Philippians 2:14–15*

Observation: A complaining spirit infects our everyday environment. At work, at home, on social media, it can be contagious. Your candidate doesn't win the election, so you blame the other party for all of society's woes. Your team doesn't win the tournament, and the referees were biased or the coach was incompetent. Your kids don't clean up after themselves. Your husband is insensitive. Your job is too demanding and the pay isn't fair. Your lunch wasn't prepared correctly. The winter was too long, but then the heat of summer comes too soon. My guess is that while reading these examples you found yourself easily agreeing, maybe even jumping to your own list of complaints!

Even God's people can easily slip into a complaining attitude, because, after all, it's not really a sin, is it? Complaining sure seems relatively harmless compared to murder, adultery, or theft. Grumbling now and then doesn't affect others like lying or jealousy.

But what we complain about reveals what really matters to us. Our grumbling has a way of exposing where our hearts are centered. Whining, in many ways, is the polar opposite of worshiping the Lord. Worship is when we glorify God for who he is and acknowledge what he has done for us, but whining is ignoring who God is and forgetting what he has done for us.

So Paul says, in effect, You want to be blameless? You want to live a pure life? You want your life to shine like a bright star on a cloudless night? Then don't grumble. Don't argue or complain. Instead of whining, try worshiping.

denying today

You won't be able to do this without God's help, but just for today make this commitment: As a follower of Jesus, do everything without grumbling or complaining. When you are tempted to whine, turn it into a moment of worship. When tempted to complain, respond instead with thanksgiving. Read a psalm, pray a prayer, turn up the worship music, and thank God for all that he has already done for you. (For a further challenge, try this for a week. Enlist a few close friends or family members to try it with you and hold you accountable.)

DAY 24

chasing after the wind

> "Utterly meaningless! Everything is meaningless." . . .
>
> All things are wearisome, more than one can say. The eye never has enough of seeing, nor the ear its fill of hearing. What has been will be again, what has been done will be done again; there is nothing new under the sun. . . .
>
> I have seen all the things that are done under the sun; all of them are meaningless, a chasing after the wind.
>
> —*Ecclesiastes 1:2, 8–9, 14*

Have you ever wondered why so many people are bored today, during an age of technological wonders, of over two hundred TV channels? Science writer Winifred Gallagher believes that boredom is largely a recent problem that is absent from many other cultures. She describes a Western anthropologist who has studied the bushmen of Namibia for years and has become fluent in their language. He has attempted over the years to come up with an equivalent word for "boredom" in their language, but there is a disconnect; they don't understand the concept. The closest they can come to it is *tired*. Our word *boredom* didn't appear in English until the Industrial Age—about the time modern entertainment began to evolve.

Wise King Solomon may not have had a word for boredom, either, but he portrayed it well with words like *meaningless* and *vanity*—"a chasing after the wind." Put this book down, go outside, and take three minutes to chase the wind. Go ahead. Are you back? How'd that go for you? What do you have to show for it?

Solomon made a relentless pursuit of pleasure and entertainment. He denied himself nothing. He enjoyed comedy and laughter, parties and projects. And at the end of it all, his conclusion was that it was all meaningless. He seems to say, "It just wears me out."

Christian writer A. W. Tozer observed that the more vibrant our inner lives are, the less we need from the outside—that is, the more active we are in mind and spirit, the less we need to fall back on external media and other input. The apostle Paul put it this way: "Offer your bodies as a living sacrifice, holy and pleasing to God—this is your true and proper worship. Do not conform to the pattern of this world, but be transformed by the renewing of your mind" (Rom. 12:1–2). We were made for God, and until he is our greatest pleasure, all the other pleasures of this life will lead to emptiness.

denying today

Think about these revealing questions: What are your favorite forms of entertainment? Where and when have you exhibited the most passion and excitement? What kinds of entertainment media have you found to be the most addictive? Decide now that the next time you feel bored, instead of turning on the TV or picking up your smartphone, you'll do something to renew your mind. (Here's a hint: *Worship* and the *Word* are both good places to start.)

DAY 25

sacrificial living

"Greater love has no one than this: to lay down one's life for one's friends."

—John 15:13

You hear about them occasionally: real-life heroes who sacrifice themselves for others. They pay the ultimate price by giving up their very lives. A soldier on the foreign battlefield. A firefighter rushing into a burning building. A concerned passerby who steps into harm's way. The stories become legends. Monuments are built with pride. It's the stuff greatness is made of.

Some of their names we know and remember; others died in obscurity. Still, they are heroes just the same.

Hebrews 11 has come to be known as the "faith chapter" of the Bible, listing mighty heroes of old like Noah, Abraham, Isaac, and Jacob. We read about Joseph and Moses. We see recognizable names like Gideon, Samson, and mighty King David.

Then we read about others. Faceless people whose names we may never know, but heroes nonetheless. We read about how they "were tortured, refusing to be released so that they might gain an even better resurrection. Some faced jeers and flogging, and even chains and imprisonment. They were put to death by stoning; they were sawed in two; they were killed by the sword. They went about in sheepskins and goatskins, destitute, persecuted and mistreated" (Heb. 11:35–37). And then we read this short commendation: "The world was not worthy of them" (v. 38).

I don't know all that Jesus will ask of you as you follow him. I don't know what denying yourself will look like in your lifetime. Forsaking pleasure, sure. Letting go of recognition and applause, quite possibly. Denying gods of lust and power? Certainly. Laying down your very life? Perhaps, I don't know. But I do know this: If your life comes to *that*, your sacrifice will be worth it. And one day, when Jesus returns, you'll be counted among those who triumph over the accuser, who "did not love their lives so much as to shrink from death" (see Rev. 12:10–11). And Jesus himself will commend you. *Well done.*

denying today

You don't have to read too many headlines to know that Christians around the world are being persecuted for their faith. Pray today for our persecuted brothers and sisters. Pray that they will sense God's presence and feel connected to the greater body of Christ. Pray for their boldness to make Christ known. Pray that they will forgive and love their persecutors. Pray that they will rejoice in suffering and be refreshed through God's Word and grow in their faith. Pray that they'll be strengthened through the prayers of fellow believers. And pray that they'll experience God's comfort when their family members are killed, injured, or imprisoned for their witness. (Consider visiting the Voice of the Martyrs website, *www.persecution.com*, for more information regarding the persecuted church.)

a prayer of denial

God, I see that in becoming like Jesus, I have to lose more of me, and eventually lose all of me, because only then will I discover the real life you have for me. I know that letting go of me and living for you is better, so much better. It's just hard. I'm comfortable with me. I'm selfish. I want what I want. I am demanding. I act entitled so easily. I twist motives so I seem really ambitious instead of conceited. My whole day can revolve around my wants, and then I'll pretend it didn't so it looks like I denied myself. I am not comfortable in denial.

In my honest moments, though, I know it's better, so I have big hopes for letting go of myself with this prayer. I need you. Will you unravel my layers of selfishness? Will you realign my deepest motives? Will you empower me to say yes and no to the right things? You say that I can deny myself because your Holy Spirit lives in me. He's powerful. I believe you. I say yes to following Jesus, so I say yes to dying to myself.

Please, God, may the entitled, wanting, comfortable, demanding, self-absorbed me become less and less so I am eventually completely lost in you.

Amen.

25 DAYS OF PURSUING

It started with a decision to follow. A response, really, to Jesus' invitation to follow him. To get to know him and to be fully known by him.

But you can't follow him completely unless you're willing to leave some things behind. "Whoever wants to be my disciple must deny themselves," Jesus said (Matt. 16:24).

And now, at this point of our journey together, we'll focus on *pursuing* Jesus. A pursuit is an activity with a specific goal and end game. It carries the idea of living *on purpose*. We demonstrate our commitment to Christ by giving our lives to his mission. We begin to see people as he saw them and to love them with his love. We live by kingdom priorities and principles. We engage in meaningful relationships and make a difference in our communities. We meet needs and serve others not because it's a civil duty or a social obligation but because it is the way Jesus lived.

Remember this: "Whoever claims to live in him must live as Jesus did" (1 John 2:6).

DAY 1

multiple choice

> "Now fear the Lord and serve him with all faithfulness. Throw away the gods your ancestors worshiped beyond the Euphrates River and in Egypt, and serve the Lord. But if serving the Lord seems undesirable to you, then choose for yourselves this day whom you will serve. . . . As for me and my household, we will serve the Lord."
>
> —*Joshua 24:14–15*

Moses led the homeless nation of Israel out of Egypt, where the people had been enslaved for several generations. God demonstrated his power through the ten plagues, the splitting of the Red Sea, and the provision of food from heaven and water from a rock. He even provided them with a supernatural GPS system by leading them with a cloud during the day and a pillar of fire at night.

But the people still didn't have much faith. They constantly whined and complained. What should have been about a monthlong hike turned into a camping trip that lasted four decades. Moses and an entire generation of those who left Egypt never even made it to the land God had promised Abraham hundreds of years earlier. Joshua replaced Moses as the leader of God's people and brought them into the Promised Land.

But before they could take possession of their new land, they had to get something squared away. Joshua, now an old man himself, gathers the people of Israel together for a farewell address. I find it interesting that he does not demand or coerce the people to follow God. In fact, he gives them three options *along with* the one true God. "Choose for yourselves," he says, "whom you will serve." Don't miss the underlying assumption: You *will* make a choice. All of us are worshipers—we are hardwired this way. The question is never, Am I a worshiper? It's always, Who or what am I worshiping?

And make no mistake: You will end up serving the god/God you have chosen. Often willfully, sometimes dutifully, perhaps even regretfully. The master always rules over the servant.

- You choose the *old* gods your parents and grandparents chose, and you find yourself bowing under the pressure of family expectations that can never be met.
- You choose the gods you met *next*, in college or out on your own, and wake up enslaved to pursuits that can never really satisfy.
- You choose the *local* gods (sexual pleasure, entertainment, success) and discover that you are just

> as defeated as the generations of people who served those gods before you.

Or you can make the choice Joshua did: "As for me and my household, we will serve the LORD." It's a choice that offers real life and maximum meaning and profound purpose. Serving the Lord truly has eternal consequence. What will you choose?

pursuing today

Our choices are a strong indication of what gods we are worshiping. Evaluate the choices you are making: what you choose to do for a living, how you manage your money, what you watch on TV, whom you befriend, what websites you visit, what you wear, what you eat, even what you choose to think about. Consider the things you will do or decide this week. What do your choices reveal about whom or what you are serving?

DAY 2

it's not too late

> Always give yourselves fully to the work of the Lord, because you know that your labor in the Lord is not in vain.
>
> *—1 Corinthians 15:58*

We all want to be difference makers—not space takers or time wasters. But if we're honest, most of us say, "It's too late now." I'm too far down my career path. I've made too many bad choices. I'm too old. I burned those bridges a long time ago. I'm carrying too much baggage. I can't break these habits. There's no way to hit rewind or click delete. It's too late now.

You may never have felt called to the mission field, but you may feel that you had some kind of opportunity and you missed it. When you sensed that God wanted you to make a difference in your neighborhood, you failed to reach out. You once made a genuine effort to meet your neighbors and learn their names, but now many of them have moved away, and it would be awkward to start over with the ones who haven't. You believed that God wanted you to be a spiritual leader in your home, but you felt inadequate. Now you see your children making bad decisions, walking away from their faith, but they're out of your home and it's too late to go back and fix your mistakes.

You don't know how to push the restart button. And like most people, not knowing what to do means you default to doing nothing. You find yourself just sitting at home.

But it's still not too late with Jesus. It's not too late to have a fresh start. Look at the apostle Paul, who used to be Saul, the Christian-killer. If it wasn't too late for Paul, it can't be too late for you and me to surrender to Jesus and then make a difference. It's not too late to quit living accidentally and start living on purpose.

"See to it, brothers and sisters, that none of you has a sinful, unbelieving heart that turns away from the living God. But encourage one another daily, as long as it is called 'Today'" (Heb. 3:12–13).

pursuing today

Name one or two things you wish you would have done differently in your life. What career would you have chosen? What opportunity would you have taken advantage of? Can you think of a time when you sensed God calling you to do something and you ignored it? Write out a prayer asking him what to do, and how. And "if you hear [God's] voice, do not harden your hearts" (Heb. 3:15). Write down what you will do *today.* Take that first step. Do *something.*

DAY 3

the heart of the issue

> Above all else, guard your heart, for everything you do flows from it.
>
> —*Proverbs 4:23*

What is your "heart"? In science, we know that it's the blood-pumping organ that makes the rest of the body run. It doesn't think; it doesn't feel. But in Hebrew culture, the heart was seen differently. It was a metaphor for the center or core of a person's personality. It was the spiritual hub, and one's life flowed from its orientation. *Everything* flowed from the heart—not only blood, but personality, motives, emotions, and will.

In Hebrew, the word for "heart" means "the kernel of the nut." Your heart reflects your true identity. Understanding this concept helps us realize why "guarding the heart" is so important. We recognize it as the source from which our thoughts, feelings, and actions flow.

Imagine the futility and frustration of trying to clean a downstream section of a creek, when all the while a garbage dump up at the creek's source is continually polluting it with load after load of filth. Sure, you could go and clean every day, but it would be like pushing a boulder up a hill only to watch it roll back down again.

How much of your life do you spend dealing with the visible garbage downstream, rather than what produces it? It's easy to focus on "behavior modification," just picking up bits of trash here and there as we see them. But that only addresses the symptoms. It's a quick-fix methodology for a long-term issue. It's like a bandage for your elbow when the issue is your heart. It's not that addressing behaviors can't yield positive results. It's simply that the heart of the issue is an issue of the heart.

We need to learn to hike upstream, with the Holy Spirit as our guide, to remedy the issue at the source. It's a staggering commitment, but it will be worth the extra effort.

pursuing today

Do some serious reflecting on these questions as a kind of "spiritual heart test": What disappoints you? What do you complain about the most? Where do you make financial sacrifices? What worries you? Where do you go when you're hurting? What infuriates you? What are your dreams? Memorize God's promise: "You will seek me and find me when you seek me with all your heart" (Jer. 29:13).

DAY 4

pots, pans, and the presence of god

> Rejoice always, pray continually, give thanks in all circumstances; for this is God's will for you in Christ Jesus.
>
> —*1 Thessalonians 5:16–18*

If the name Brother Lawrence sounds familiar, it's not because he's Joey's brother. He was a medieval monk who served in the monastery kitchen, and he learned to "practice the presence of God" as he scrubbed the pots and pans.

As much as I admire Brother Lawrence's commitment, doing the dishes has never been much of a devotional time for me. The reality is that I have to be intentional to schedule time to be still in the presence of God. For me it means setting aside time every morning to surrender my thoughts, my desires, and my plans to God. I can't coast on yesterday's successes or live paralyzed by yesterday's failures. I make a daily choice to pursue God, knowing that "if I seek him, I will find him" (see Matt. 7:7–8).

But here's the key: When my scheduled time with God comes to an end, I don't say to God, "Goodbye," "See you later," or "Talk to you tomorrow"; instead, I accept his invitation to walk with him throughout the day. I tell him I want to keep the conversation going. I try to intentionally keep talking and listening as I drive to work, attend meetings, and, on occasion, clean the kitchen. I *practice his presence* and anticipate his faithful attentiveness to my prayers.

I can't treat my daily time with God like I treat a physical workout, where once it's complete I check it off until the next day. Instead, I try to think of my daily time alone with God as a sort of "spiritual workout" in order to run the day's race effectively, with more peace and joy than I could ever find running alone. Think of it this way: Start your prayer in the morning, and don't say "amen" until you're falling asleep at night.

pursuing today

If you haven't already done so, schedule a daily "workout" time, even if you can dedicate only five or ten minutes at first. For the next several days, consider starting your day by reading Psalm 63:1–8. Read it aloud, making it your prayer. Then see if you can find ways to exercise the muscles of your spirit throughout the day.

DAY 5

god-breathed

> The Holy Scriptures . . . are able to make you wise for salvation through faith in Christ Jesus. All Scripture is God-breathed and is useful for teaching, rebuking, correcting and training in righteousness, so that the servant of God may be thoroughly equipped for every good work.
>
> *—2 Timothy 3:15–17*

Have you ever walked down the hall of a college music school in the late afternoon, past the closed practice room doors? If you have, you may have wanted to cover your ears. Each musician is practicing a different song on a different instrument. The result is a discordant cacophony. Piano scales clash against trombone solos; cellos duel with tubas. The music doesn't seem to belong together.

The Bible can seem like that. As you turn the pages, you encounter a little bit of everything. Blood-splattered war chronicles. Polite correspondence. Twisting tales of intrigue and betrayal. Lyrical poetry. Thundering prophecies. Tedious legal records. Desperate cries for help. Sensual love songs. If you're looking for one unified presentation, you might become disenchanted in a hurry. Sometimes it feels as if all you can hear is clashing notes.

Yet, Timothy wrote, every word of the Bible is God-breathed. Every chapter is helpful; every refrain useful. Whether you're moved by the honest lyrics of the Psalms or stunned by the merciless admonishments of Obadiah. Whether captivated by the adventurous missions of Paul or depressed by the laments of Job. Whether embarrassed by the explicit Song of Songs or inspired by the very words of Jesus. The goal of it all is to train you to live like Jesus, walk with him, and join him on his mission.

So pause to listen, one book, chapter, or verse at a time. But don't stop with listening; respond in obedience to what you have heard. You'll find that the more you respond to what you hear, the more you will hear. And as you respond, you'll discover that you are "thoroughly equipped for every good work" that God has already planned for you to accomplish.

pursuing today

Open up your Bible and begin reading it. Not sure where to start? Download a Bible app on your smartphone and choose one of hundreds of good reading plans. But start today. As you read, consider keeping a journal handy so you can record what you hear God saying to you. At the risk of sounding cheesy, your obedience will be music to Jesus' ears.

DAY 6

leave your bible open

Man does not live on bread alone but on every word that comes from the mouth of the LORD.

—Deuteronomy 8:3

Daily Bible reading is a habit worth developing. The Word feeds us spiritually and satisfies our thirst for peace. It convicts us of sin and reminds us of God's grace. Still, the Bible will not jump into your hands or demand your attention. Chances are nobody will be checking up on whether you spent time in the Scriptures today. Yet few things could possibly be more important.

According to the American Bible Society, more than half of the population would like to read the Bible more often, but only 15 percent of Americans do it daily. Southerners and the elderly do it the best. (So if you're an elderly Southerner, you get a free pass to skip to the next devotion.)

Most of us would cite the same reason for not spending daily time in our Bibles: "I'm just too busy." But are we? I don't mean to get too nosy, but how much time did you spend on Facebook or Pinterest today? How often did you check your Instagram feed or scan the latest Groupon deals? How long did you park yourself in front of your TV or gaming console? We find plenty of time to scan today's news headlines or devour our newest novel. Yet we ignore the very words—the only words—that have the power of life.

What you feed yourself is what you start to develop an appetite for. God's Word will appeal to you more and more as you learn to turn away from competing interests. In other words, you may have to subtract something in order to add Bible reading to your day. But you'll find the trade to be well worth it.

pursuing today

To help develop a new habit, plan to read your Bible (even for a few minutes) at the same time and in the same location every day. Leave your Bible open or set an alarm to remind you. Try it for the remainder of this twenty-five-day section. If you have some extra time, read Psalm 119, an entire psalm devoted to the power of God's Word. Notice all the different names for God's Word—laws, statutes, etc. Then make note of all the benefits of spending time in it.

DAY 7

every knee

Therefore God exalted him to the highest place and gave him the name that is above every name, that at the name of Jesus every knee should bow, in heaven and on earth and under the earth, and every tongue acknowledge that Jesus Christ is Lord, to the glory of God the Father.

—*Philippians 2:9–11*

The older I get, the more attention I pay to my knees. I used to give them no thought at all, except maybe when I skinned one as a kid or injured one playing basketball. But now I'm aware of the relentless wear and tear they suffer, and I don't take them for granted. As the largest joints in the human body, they are sturdy enough to support me when I stand up, and also flexible enough to bend with every step I take. I command my knee to move with enough strength to kick a ball, yet I can't control an involuntary reflex to the light touch of a well-placed hammer.

My knees also make it possible for me to *kneel* down to pray on the floor next to my bed each night or in my closet as I start each morning. And this outward physical posture is a reflection of an inward spiritual one: A bowed knee demonstrates a humble heart.

Carl Jung, the famous psychotherapist, used to tell a story about a rabbi. Someone asked the rabbi, "Why did God often show himself to people in ancient times, but today, no one ever sees him?" The wise rabbi answered, "Because now no one bends low enough to see God."

Jesus modeled this posture perfectly for us. The apostle Paul writes that even though Jesus could have used his God-nature to his own advantage, "he made himself nothing" and humbled himself even to the point of death on a cross (see Phil. 2:6–8). He didn't play his "God card." He stepped down to take on human form, and then he knelt further in the posture of a servant. And when he did, God exalted him.

We are called to this mindset as well. As God's sons and daughters in this self-sufficient age, let's be countercultural. Let's value others above ourselves because we value Christ above all. Together and individually, let's bend low enough so that we too can get a glimpse of God.

Standing proudly in the presence of someone who is greater will never get us very far. In fact, "God opposes the proud but shows favor to the humble" (1 Peter 5:5). Our pursuit of God should always begin on our knees.

pursuing today

Read Philippians 2:1–4, highlighting or underlining phrases that describe a humble posture toward others. Pray about some practical ways you can "look to the interests of others" today. Write them down, and commit to doing them. An additional thought: For some of you, getting on your knees to pray will feel more than just physically uncomfortable. There is something humbling about it, and that's the point. Find a quiet place, get on your knees, and ask God for help. Begin your prayer with these three simple words: "I need you . . ."

DAY 8

the least of these

> The King will reply, "Truly I tell you, whatever you did for one of the least of these brothers and sisters of mine, you did for me."
>
> —*Matthew 25:40*

Jesus tells a story in Matthew 25 that haunts me from time to time. Though it follows a string of parables, this story is not one. It's a straightforward depiction of what will take place when Jesus comes to this earth again.

On that day, Jesus will separate everybody in the world into two groups—the righteous "sheep" on his right and the wicked "goats" on his left. He'll tell them two slightly different versions of the same story. To the sheep: When I was hungry and thirsty, you fed me. When I was a stranger, you were hospitable and invited me into your house. When I needed some clothes, you gave me a couple of shirts and a nice pair of pants. That time I was sick? You nursed me to health. That time I was put in prison? You showed up during visiting hours.

Those listening will be more than a little confused. "When did we see you like this?" they'll ask. "We never knew you were hungry or thirsty. When did we see you a stranger or without clothes? We don't remember you being sick or in prison and coming to visit you. When did we meet these needs?" The sheep wait for an answer, scratching their heads and exchanging puzzled looks.

Finally, Jesus breaks the silence and replies: "Whatever you did for one of the least of these brothers and sisters of mine, you did for me" (Matt. 25:40). This crowd smiles and exhales in unison. Then Jesus rewards them with a blessing—an inheritance in his kingdom.

But to those on his left, he gives a scathing rebuke: I was hungry and thirsty, and you couldn't even scrounge up any leftovers. I was a stranger, and you looked right past me. I didn't have any clothes, and you couldn't find anything to spare out of your overflowing closets. I was sick, and you turned a blind eye. I was in prison, and you just wrote me off as someone else's problem.

The goats squirm nervously. They too respond, in an almost defensive, desperate tone: "We never saw you like that . . . did we? When did that happen? When did we not meet your needs? If only we'd known it was you!"

And Jesus replies: "Whatever you did not do for one of the least of these, you did not do for me" (Matt. 25:45). Then the goats are sent away for eternal punishment.

It's a simple story making an obvious point. You and I *will* have opportunities to see Jesus; you are probably realizing now that you already have. Maybe you saw him today as you drove to work. Maybe he keeps to himself in the cubicle just down the row from you. Maybe he lives next door to you. Maybe you read about his arrest in the paper.

So when you see him, will you recognize him? And perhaps more important, will you respond by serving him?

pursuing today

The application is clear. Keep your eyes open for opportunities to serve "the least of these." Ignore the excuses that pull at you ("He'll probably spend my money on alcohol," "She got herself into this mess," "He's just really difficult to love"). Serve. Give. Love. For Christ's sake, don't miss your opportunity.

DAY 9

freedom of choice

> The people answered, "Far be it from us to forsake the LORD to serve other gods! . . . We too will serve the LORD, because he is our God."
>
> —*Joshua 24:16, 18*

Christian philosopher Peter Kreeft says, "The opposite of theism is not atheism. It's idolatry." Everyone is going to worship a god of some sort (yes, even atheists), because we were created to be worshipers. It's written into our genetic code. It's an inescapable part of our job description as human beings. Worship comes as factory-installed, standard equipment in any member of the human race who has a body, a mind, and emotions.

The question, of course, is whom or what you will *choose* to worship personally. There are lots of options, and most of them are not "religious." In whom or what do you put your hope? What do you pursue? In short, to what do you give the bulk of your life's attention?

Here are some choices that reveal the god or gods you may be worshiping:

- How you spend your day off or your free time
- Whom you choose as friends and which ones you call in a crisis

- What you do for a living
- How you manage your money
- What you watch on TV or what websites you visit
- What clothes you wear (or wish you could afford to wear)
- What food you eat
- What you think about
- How you spend your Sundays
- What type and level of education you are getting or have gotten
- Whether or not you have a time apart with God—every day of the week

Instead of worrying about the question, "What god am I serving?" look at your choices. You really are free to choose. But choosing well can be difficult.

pursuing today

Ask yourself, What choices am I making? Have I been influenced by the choices of my friends and family? The culture around me? Consider your answers to the choices listed above. Stop for a moment and weigh your options. Then complete these sentences, using the same language the people of Israel used. "Far be it from us to forsake the Lord to serve [blank]. We too will serve the Lord because [blank]."

DAY 10

outsider

"I will ask the Father, and he will give you another advocate to help you and be with you forever."

—*John 14:16*

I married a girl from a small Kansas town. How small? Well, directions to her house include the following: "Turn right at the wagon wheel next to the dirt road." She grew up on a farm several miles down that very road. Whenever we show up for a visit, her family tries to make me feel welcome, but I can almost hear that old Sesame Street song in the background: "One of these things is not like the other. One of these things just doesn't belong."

One Thanksgiving, the men of the family, dressed to kill (literally) in camo, slipped out of the house, ready to go hunting after the big meal. About a half hour later, I realized I was the only grown man in the house. I walked into the kitchen, where the ladies were making pies, and asked, "Do you know where the men went?" My mother-in-law said, and I quote, "All the men are outside." Um . . . hello? Clearly they weren't *all* outside. Apparently they'd left on their four-wheelers to go build a deer stand together, but no one had thought to invite me. Now, I know they believe in my existence. I would say that most of them like me and perhaps even respect me. But they aren't quite sure what to do with me.

This is how a lot of Christians approach the Holy Spirit. To them, he is sort of like the Cousin Eddie of the Trinity—the one you're not quite sure how to relate to. It never occurs to some of us that he (not "it," by the way) may be our vital link to the Father and Jesus. We promise ourselves and others that we're really going to change this time. But the change lasts only a few days. We keep striving to obey Jesus' commands on our own, as if it were somehow possible to actually love our enemies, forgive those who have hurt us, or consistently consider others better than ourselves. On our own, it just doesn't work. When we try to pursue Jesus without being filled daily with the Spirit, we find ourselves frustrated by our failures and exhausted by our efforts.

Here's the bad news: You cannot live the life Jesus calls you to in your own strength. But here's the good news: You were never meant to. And here's even better news: For the Christian, the power of God's Holy Spirit is already available inside of you. Begin discovering the Spirit's power by asking God to give it to you today and then paying attention to the ways it shows up in your life. It may manifest as extra patience with a family member, or an unusual amount of self-control with a temptation, or maybe you will experience a supernatural sense of peace in the midst of an overwhelming difficulty. God has given you this gift; make sure you open it.

pursuing today

What life circumstances are currently overwhelming you? What areas of your life are you trying to manage on your own? What promises have you made again that you have failed to keep *again*? (Be honest here; put words to your weaknesses and write them down.) Now compare your list to the fruit of the Spirit found in Galatians 5:22–23. Identify where the power of the Holy Spirit can give you victory, and begin to surrender to him daily.

DAY 11

moving sidewalk

"The Spirit gives life; the flesh counts for nothing. The words I have spoken to you—they are full of the Spirit and life."

—*John 6:63*

My family and I flew into the Atlanta airport after a monthlong mission trip to the island of Hispaniola. After landing, we grabbed our bags and began the long hike to our connecting gate. When we travel, my wife and I split the luggage responsibilities: One of us packs lots of stuff, and one of us carries it everywhere. That's how we've worked it out. So I'm carrying about a half dozen bags through the airport. They're hanging all over me. It's just a moving pile of bags with my head sticking out the top. We turn to go down a hallway that is about a hundred yards long. My wife and kids all get on a moving sidewalk. But carrying my wide load, I'm not able to navigate the turn and I miss the on-ramp. I wish you could have seen what it looked like from my perspective. They set the few bags they have on the moving sidewalk and just stand there watching me. I'm sweating like, well, like a man carrying a half dozen suitcases through an airport. I'm trying to keep up with the pace. We end up arriving at the end of the side-walk at about the same time, but there's a difference. I'm frustrated, exhausted, and annoyed, and they are ready to keep moving.

That's what our lives look like when we try the self-empowered hike instead of the Spirit-filled walkway. You can try to play the role of the Holy Spirit, but trying to be God has a tendency to wear you out.

Jesus knew that would happen. So he promised to give us an advocate to help us and be with us (see John 14:15–17). His Spirit teaches us, gives us life, guides us into truth, convicts us of sin, and reminds us of what Jesus said. He gives powerful gifts that we could never manufacture on our own. And he always, always points us to Jesus.

pursuing today

Do a quick search with your Bible app or an online Bible version (or a good old-fashioned concordance) for the word *Spirit*. Look up several of the first verses that come up. Using short phrases—two or three words—write down several observations about the activity of God's Spirit. What are some ways you have experienced that active presence in your own life as you pursue him?

DAY 12

exhale, inhale

> Since we live by the Spirit, let us keep in step with the Spirit.
>
> —*Galatians 5:25*

The teaching of Bill Bright, cofounder of Campus Crusade for Christ (now Cru), has helped me learn to become a follower of Christ who is filled with the Spirit. He taught a spiritual exercise called "spiritual breathing." The basic idea is that you learn to live with a moment-by-moment awareness of the Spirit until walking in the Spirit becomes as natural as breathing. It's just part of who you are.

Here's how it works: The moment you become aware of an area of sin in your life, you *exhale*. When you exhale, you breathe out the impurity of your sin and repent of it. Repentance becomes a natural response, clearing out space in your heart for the Spirit to fill you. The moment you become prideful, jealous, lustful, harsh, selfish, dishonest, impatient, etc.—you *exhale* and repent on the spot.

And then you *inhale*. You breathe in and pray to be filled with the Spirit. You surrender control to him. You thank him for forgiving you, and you receive the purity and fullness of the Holy Spirit. You let him empower and direct you.

As you practice this spiritual breathing, it teaches you to keep in step with the Spirit. It will probably seem unnatural at first. Your first few tries will be self-conscious and you will feel like a toddler learning to walk. It will take your total concentration. But before long, you will be putting one foot in front of the other and walking will feel completely natural.

Spiritual breathing is an exercise of your faith, and it enables you to experience God's love and forgiveness on an ongoing basis.

pursuing today

Starting right now, try this simple exercise. Exhale. (What do you need to confess? In what ways are you still striving to live in your own power?) Inhale. (Surrender yourself again to the work and power of the Holy Spirit inside of you.) Repeat. Give him room. Let the Spirit breathe through you.

DAY 13

holy comforter

> Praise be to the God and Father of our Lord Jesus Christ, the Father of compassion and the God of all comfort, who comforts us in all our troubles, so that we can comfort those in any trouble with the comfort we ourselves receive from God. For just as we share abundantly in the sufferings of Christ, so also our comfort abounds through Christ.
>
> —*2 Corinthians 1:3–5*

In a museum in northern France, you can view the Bayeaux Tapestry. It is so long that it wraps around the walls of a large room, like the longest cartoon strip ever, with hundreds of scenes and captions. It dates from the late eleventh century and tells the story of the Norman Conquest. The Latin captions were first translated into English in the seventeenth century.

One scene depicts William the Conqueror urging his troops forward into a bloody battle at lance-point. The caption on the panel is translated, "William comforts his soldiers." Pushing them into battle. Urging them on with the tip of his blade. Something must have been lost in translation, right? But this is not a mistake. The translation was made around the time when Bibles were first coming out in English, giving us the term *Comforter* for the Holy Spirit, and *comfort* had a different meaning than it does now.

So why am I telling you this? Because these days, when we think of a comforter, we think of a nice soft blanket. We want to stay in our comfort zones, take comfort measures, and eat comfort food. We enjoy creature comforts like comfortable homes and comfy clothes. But the word really means "with great strength." It carries the idea of en*courage*ment in the strongest sense of the word, because it includes the idea of pressing someone to take an action that could mean *dis*comfort. When you think of the Holy Spirit, put warm fuzzies aside.

Yes, he will come alongside you to comfort you in your grief. He is more than capable of giving you peace that is not dependent on your circumstances. But the Comforter also might shake you up and dislodge you from your safe and comfortable rut, especially when a battle rages just ahead.

pursuing today

How have you experienced the Holy Spirit? Recall the times he has stimulated you and strengthened you to face challenges. How has his comfort both calmed you and given you strength? In your own words, contrast the pursuit of *comfort* with the pursuit of *the Comforter.*

DAY 14

walk the walk

So I say, walk by the Spirit.

—*Galatians 5:16*

When you took your first steps as a baby, everyone praised you. But that was not your crowning achievement as a biped, because you went on to run, skip, jump, and dance. Nobody praises the nine-year-old boy for walking across the living room into his mother's open arms. No one cheers as the forty-two-year-old woman navigates her way around the dining room by holding on to the edge of the table. Learning to walk was just a normal part of growing up.

Over the years, sometimes your feet have taken you places you weren't supposed to go. You directed your own steps according to your objectives, often influenced by the people you were walking with. Sometimes you walked in the dark and it was difficult to see where you were going. Sometimes you ran right into trouble. Other times you strolled in the sunshine and everything was good.

You have been on a parallel path in your spiritual walk. You took your first steps when you were saved, but that was only the beginning of your journey. Sometimes you stumbled in the dark, losing your way. Other times you took a deliberate detour and found yourself alone. But many times you followed closely in the footsteps of Jesus. You "kept [your] feet from every evil path" (Ps. 119:101); you chose to "run in the path of [his] commands" (Ps. 119:32). And you discovered the beautiful truth that "blessed are those whose ways are blameless, who walk according to the law of the LORD" (Ps. 119:1).

That's being a disciple. That's pursuing Jesus. And the more the two of you walk together, the more you walk the way he does.

pursuing today

Can you see maturing fruit in your life? That's the best way to know if you have progressed from baby steps to mature strides. If you haven't already, memorize this scripture: "But the fruit of the Spirit is love, joy, peace, forbearance, kindness, goodness, faithfulness, gentleness and self-control. . . . Since we live by the Spirit, let us keep in step with the Spirit" (Gal. 5:22–23, 25). List that "fruit" on a note card and put it in an obvious place where you will see it each day.

DAY 15

in this together

> Therefore encourage one another and build each other up, just as in fact you are doing.
>
> —*1 Thessalonians 5:11*

I have a friend who recently participated in a five-mile mud run. Now, this is not one of those "I have a friend who" stories that is meant to mask the fact that I'm secretly referring to me. Honestly, just that first sentence tells you pretty much everything you need to know about why such an event holds no appeal for me. Three words (or four, depending on how you count the hyphen): Five-mile. Mud. Run.

I listened as he described the obstacle course: miles of running over muddy terrain (that's the obvious part), scaling walls, climbing ropes, dragging boulders, heaving sandbags, crawling under barbed-wire fencing, and jumping over a fiery pit at the finish line. All that for a pretty cool medal and a free banana.

It wasn't necessarily a stretch for me to picture my friend running this race. I know him well: He's a pretty active guy and in reasonably good shape. He's fairly athletic, and he's *very* competitive. My surprise registered only when he told me he had completed the race right alongside his wife. I also know her well: While he is competitive, she is contented. Where he would enjoy taking a risk, she would prefer going on a retreat. He spent four to five days a week training at the gym; she spent forty-five dollars on her race outfit. She *would* not have even signed up without his gentle insistence; and she admitted that she *could* not have finished without his strong assistance. Along with two other married couples, they had run this rugged race and crossed the finish line *together*.

It occurred to me that maybe that was the whole point of the race. To compete *together*. To strive *together*. To celebrate *together*. And maybe that's the point of our journey too. The writer of Ecclesiastes wisely recognizes that "two are better than one, because they have a good return for their labor: If either of them falls down, one can help the other up. But pity anyone who falls and has no one to help them up" (Eccl. 4:9–10). We were meant to run life's race *together*.

- To encourage each other (1 Thess. 5:11).
- To pray for one another (James 5:16).
- To challenge and sharpen each other (Prov. 27:17).
- To share others' burdens and meet their needs (Gal. 6:2).
- To suffer together and to rejoice together (1 Cor. 12:26).

The race can get long; obstacles will certainly come. So "let *us* run with perseverance the race marked out for *us*, fixing *our* eyes on Jesus" (Heb. 12:1–2, emphasis added). Pursuing Jesus is always better *together*.

pursuing today

Who are the people in your life running alongside you? How do they encourage you or build you up? Who are you pouring your life into, cheering them on along the way? Write down some names, and thank God for your faith community. Consider writing a note of thanks or encouragement to someone on your list. If you find it hard to think of names, begin praying that God would lead you to some life-giving relationships.

DAY 16

pull on the rope

Bear with each other and forgive one another if any of you has a grievance against someone. Forgive as the Lord forgave you.

—*Colossians 3:13*

You may recognize the name ten Boom. As a teenager, I read Corrie ten Boom's famous autobiography, *The Hiding Place.* Corrie's family was instrumental in hiding many Jews in their home during the Nazi invasion of the Netherlands. But eventually she was captured and imprisoned at the Ravensbrück concentration camp, where she was forced to do backbreaking labor. Years later, after the end of the war and her release, she was greeted by one of her prison guards at the end of a public meeting. With the love of Christ deeply rooted in her, she managed to forgive the guard. She noted, however, that sin, even though it is erased by forgiveness, still has repercussions. She compared it to pulling on the rope in a bell tower. When you stop, the bell keeps ringing for a while. That's like the momentum of your emotions when you have been wronged. Over time, God can heal the raw wound, but for a while, you must bear the reminder of it.

You've probably heard much about God's forgiveness—how he sent his Son to die on the cross so that we can be forgiven for our sins. We are fervent believers in receiving forgiveness. We are grateful that we have been forgiven.

But many times we have a hard time extending forgiveness to others. A drunk driver crosses the median, slamming into the bus that was carrying your child. Forgive *him*?

Your spouse betrays and deserts you. Forgive *her*? Your teenage son sneaks off with your car and wrecks it. Your neighbor takes you to court over a property dispute. Forgive *them*? What they did seems unforgivable. The wrong you've suffered is just too great to bear.

But that's exactly the point of forgiveness. We're not meant to carry that burden. We're not meant to live imprisoned by our own desire to right the wrong. Lack of forgiveness is that "bitter root" that "grows up to cause trouble and defile many" (Heb. 12:15). I've seen it, and it's not pretty. Decades of pain and separation because of stubborn unforgiveness. Families torn apart. Adult children who haven't talked to their fathers in years.

But I've also seen the beauty and freedom that come when we forgive. Marriages restored and even strengthened. Families reunited. Broken teenagers overwhelmed by the patient forgiveness of their loving parents. Oh, you may still feel the effects of the original wrong. You might still hear the bell ringing for a while. But the freedom won by forgiveness is worth it. So go ahead: Give that rope a pull.

pursuing today

As you read today, what came to mind that was (or is) hard for you to forgive? Are you still nursing any grudges? Read Jesus' parable about an unforgiving servant in Matthew 18:21–35. Prayerfully consider the next step you need to take to begin the healing process. Write a note, make a phone call, walk across the street or into the next room. And forgive just as you have been forgiven.

DAY 17

i believe

> What good is it, my brothers and sisters, if someone claims to have faith but has no deeds?
>
> *—James 2:14*

Anyone who works out at a gym several times a week will have noticed the "gym rats"—the ones who always seem to be there. At my gym you can typically spot them walking aimlessly around the weight room and staring at themselves in the mirror. But I've noticed something about these guys. They tend to have huge, well-developed upper bodies and puny little legs. This is because they spend hours working on their chests, biceps, and triceps but for the most part ignore their calves and thighs. They look like they're completely out of balance, like they might tip over on uneven terrain. It's what I call (not to their faces, of course) the "Pee-Wee Schwarzenegger" effect. They have a Schwarzenegger upper body and a Pee-Wee lower body.

Some churches (and Christians) have this same unbalanced approach when it comes to discipleship. We spend too much of our time and effort bringing people to a point of belief without clearly helping them to follow. Too often, we have written BELIEVE in big, bold capital letters. And then everything that has to do with living for Jesus and being a disciple has been put in small print: follow.

As a result, many people have made a very real decision to believe in Jesus, but they have never made a commitment to follow him. They don't know how to engage in a daily pursuit of Christ. They give a puzzled look when you describe "missional living" or "walking as Jesus walked." Unless somebody tells them, they may never know that Christian belief is more than just accepting something as fact in your mind or raising your hand and repeating the right words during an altar call.

Jesus' own brother James discussed this balance in his book in the New Testament. He asks the question above—"What good is it?"—and the answer seems obvious: It's not much good at all! But in case you didn't come to the same conclusion, he states it even more clearly: "Faith by itself, if it is not accompanied by action, is dead" (James 2:17). Believing Jesus implies movement.

Of course, biblical belief *is* the acceptance of something as real and true. But it is so much more than that. Beyond intellectual assent and heartfelt acknowledgment comes the decision to follow, and that will change the way you live the rest of your life.

pursuing today

How has your belief in Jesus manifested itself in your pursuit of him? In other words, what are you *doing* that demonstrates your belief? You can't follow and stay where you are at the same time. Our beliefs are validated by our actions. Read the rest of James 2:14–26. Prayerfully look for opportunities today to put your belief into action.

DAY 18

true lies

"Many who are first will be last, and many who are last will be first."

—*Matthew 19:30*

There are certain lies we live by. If we knew they were lies, we certainly wouldn't live by them. But there are lies that we have believed to be true, and the truth is that lies we *believe* to be true can have power over us as if they were true.

For example, we eat carrots and we encourage our kids to eat carrots because—as everyone knows—carrots improve your . . . ? Yeah, carrots improve your vision. Except that they don't. This lie is actually rooted in World War II propaganda. I know that many of you reading this right now don't believe me, but it's true. Now millions of children and adults eat carrots in hopes of improving their vision. It's not true, but because we believe it is, we end up living by the lie. Or how about this one: Many of us were told as children that we couldn't go swimming right after we ate. I remember very well getting out of the pool, going in for a snack, and then being told I had to wait at least twenty minutes before swimming again. My mother explained to me that swimming after eating is dangerous because it increases your risk of muscle cramps. Yeah, except that it doesn't. That's simply not true.

Sometimes we believe these statements because they have been so widely accepted. Nearly everyone you know believes it is true, so it must be true. Or you've believed it for such a long time, you can't imagine it could be false. You likely heard it for the first time when you were a kid, and the longer you believe something, the truer it seems.

The Bible is full of widely held beliefs that Jesus turns completely upside down. For example, you want to find real life? Then be willing to lose yours (Luke 9:23–25). You want to experience complete freedom? Then choose a life of submission (Rom. 6:19). Greatness? It's found in humbly serving others (Matt. 20:26–28). True riches? They're not accumulated in this life (Matt. 6:19–20). Somehow you can rejoice in suffering (1 Peter 4:13); you can have nothing yet possess everything (2 Cor. 6:10).

The way of Jesus may seem counterintuitive. It might feel upside down. But you can always count on the One who *is* Truth.

pursuing today

Look up these verses: Luke 6:27–28; Acts 20:35; Romans 12:17, 19; Galatians 2:20; Philippians 3:7–8; James 1:2–4. Write down the upside-down ways of Jesus that you observe. Underline one or two that you will live out today. If you have more time, read the other passages referenced in today's devotion.

DAY 19

our present sufferings

I consider that our present sufferings are not worth comparing with the glory that will be revealed in us.

—*Romans 8:18*

Chronic pain. Unrelenting poverty. Sheer loneliness. Unremitting anxieties. What if this present suffering, whatever it may be, goes on for the rest of your life? How will you handle it? Should you continue to fight against every discomfort, unfairness, and heartache? Will it ever end?

We already know this life isn't going to be easy, but heaven puts everything into perspective. Jesus said, "In this world you will have trouble. But take heart! I have overcome the world" (John 16:33).

It may be hard to imagine, but once you are in heaven, your current sufferings won't matter to you anymore. What will a mere seventy-two years of sorrow and pain look like after you have spent a million years in the presence of God himself? Once you are with him, you will have no more mourning. No kind of pain—not physical or emotional or spiritual or relational. No sicknesses at all. Not even a single tear. As Teresa of Avila said, "In the light of heaven, the worst sufferings on this earth will be seen to be no more serious than one night in an inconvenient hotel."

Pursuing Jesus happens best when we keep our eyes fixed on the end goal. The apostle Paul suffered much in his life, but he had this focused perspective: "One thing I do: Forgetting what is behind and straining toward what is ahead, I press on toward the goal to win the prize for which God has called me heavenward in Christ Jesus" (Phil. 3:13–14).

I am not trying to provide a pat, "religious" answer to whatever issue looms largest in your life at the moment. Nor am I trying to convince you that your situation should feel easy in comparison to someone else's staggering circumstances. It's just that if you want to receive genuine hope and perseverance from God, the quickest way to be strengthened by his grace is to look straight into his glory.

pursuing today

Go ahead and identify your present suffering(s). Don't discount it or compare it to others; just acknowledge what you are "straining" through now. Now read Revelation 21:1–5. Receive God's "trustworthy and true" promise for those who trust in him. Hold your present suffering up into the blinding, pain-alleviating, refining light of heaven. Can you see it anymore?

DAY 20

spiritual apathy

"I know your deeds, that you are neither cold nor hot. I wish you were either one or the other! So, because you are lukewarm—neither hot nor cold—I am about to spit you out of my mouth."

—*Revelation 3:15–16*

Several years ago, I did some research on what are known as the "Seven Deadly Sins." They don't appear as a list anywhere in Scripture, and I was curious to know how the list developed. It turns out that years ago, when the literacy rate was low and people weren't reading the Bible for themselves, some early church leaders got together and made a list of the worst sins. At least people would know what *not* to do, right?

One of the sins on the list always seemed out of place to me. "Sloth" is listed as a deadly sin. It just never seemed that deadly to me. I've always thought of sloth as laziness. You know, not changing the channel on the TV because you lost the remote and walking over to the TV would be too taxing. But I discovered that a better way to convey what the early church leaders were getting at would be to translate the original word as "spiritual apathy." It's reaching a point where you know that God loves you and that Jesus died on the cross for your sins, but you shrug your shoulders because you just don't care.

What do you do if you like the idea of pursuing Jesus, but your heart is just not in it? You used to experience zeal for Christ, but now you feel apathetic and indifferent. The good news has become old news, and the miraculous seems ordinary. How do you rekindle the old flame?

When a married couple's feelings have started to fade, the best thing they can do is to start pursuing each other the way they used to. He buys her flowers; she writes him love letters. She dresses up for him; he takes her out on dates. As they *come after* each other with extravagant and sacrificial acts of love and devotion, the feelings and passion will start to return.

That's a great place to start in your relationship with Christ. Confess your spiritual apathy; then start doing the things you did at first. John's revelation from Jesus issues a loving warning for us. If you've forsaken your first love (see Rev. 2:4–5), if you're feeling ho-hum or even somewhat bored in your pursuit of Jesus, it's time to stir up the passion.

pursuing today

Does this ring true for you? Decide this minute to do something about it. Get on your knees next to your bed and talk to God about your day. Turn on some worship music in your car and sing along. Grab a one-year Bible and start reading. Go back to your local church and surround yourself with passionate followers. Find a place to serve. "Repent and do the things you did at first" (Rev. 2:5).

DAY 21

your weakness is strong

For Christ's sake, I delight in weaknesses, in insults, in hardships, in persecutions, in difficulties. For when I am weak, then I am strong.

—*2 Corinthians 12:10*

The apostle Paul made the statement above, and we all know how he was converted on the road to Damascus. In one blinding moment (literally), he was changed from being a Christian-killer to an evangelist, and for the rest of his life he suffered greatly for the cause of Christ. He rose far above his arrogant and vicious past, pouring himself out for the sake of the gospel. He learned to delight in his hardships, because they made it possible for him to lean hard on God's strength for everything.

Chuck Colson was a kind of modern-day Paul. Before he founded Prison Fellowship, he was the last person you would expect to be converted. As Special Counsel to President Richard Nixon, he was known as a ruthless and corrupt hatchet man. He ended up in prison for his part in the Watergate cover-up, and it was there that he came to know Jesus.

Once, preaching at a Christian college commencement, he said:

> The great paradox of my life is that every time I walk into a prison and see the faces of men or women who have been transformed by the power of the living God, I realize that the thing God has chosen to use in my life is none of the successes, achievements, degrees, awards, honors, or cases I won before the Supreme Court. That's not what God is using in my life. What God is using in my life to touch the lives of literally thousands of other people is the fact that I was a convict and went to prison. That was my great defeat, the only thing in my life I didn't succeed in.

Chuck understood what Paul did, that "[God's] power is made perfect in weakness" (2 Cor. 12:9). He understood that losing everything was okay, that it was maybe even necessary to experience the "surpassing worth of knowing Christ Jesus" (Phil. 3:8). And he experienced the same "delight" that Paul experienced—a front-row seat to the power of God in the weakness of his people. Just wait 'til you see what he can do through you.

pursuing today

You and I may not have such dramatic testimonies, but we are definitely weak. What's your "great defeat" or current hardship? What insult or difficulty are you currently enduring? Write it down. Then draw a line through it—cross it out. And prayerfully imagine how God's strength will be clearly seen through your weakness.

DAY 22

when jesus says *not* to follow

> The man from whom the demons had gone out begged to go with him, but Jesus sent him away, saying, "Return home and tell how much God has done for you." So the man went away and told all over town how much Jesus had done for him.
>
> —*Luke 8:38–39*

Sometimes Jesus says *not* to follow him. Let me explain.

In Luke 8 we meet a man who is off-the-charts crazy. He is certifiably out of his right mind. Luke records that he had been running around naked and homeless for a long time. He spent most of his time in the cemetery just up the way from a very frightened group of townspeople. They tried chaining him up, but his demonically acquired strength was too much. Perhaps the only grace was that the demons drove him into solitary places.

And then Jesus invades his personal space. Their encounter is fairly brief. The legion of screaming demons is no match for Jesus, much like Richard Simmons is not in the same league as Chuck Norris. (By the way, have you heard that when Alexander Graham Bell invented the telephone, he had three missed calls from Chuck Norris? Or that when Chuck Norris enters a room, he doesn't turn the lights on, he turns the dark off? I could keep going, but I won't.) The confrontation is a "no contest" before it even begins. Jesus drives out the demons, and the man is restored—sitting peacefully, dressed modestly, and thinking rightly.

As you might imagine, he is overcome with gratitude. He is eager to spend more time with this powerful healer. He begs for the privilege of going with Jesus, but Jesus says no and sends him away with a mission: "Return home and tell how much God has done for you" (Luke 8:39). The very next phrase of that same verse records his immediate, complete obedience: "So the man went away and told all over town how much Jesus had done for him."

Sometimes Jesus says *not* to follow him. A Jesus follower is obedient above all else, so when Jesus himself tells you to go home, that's what he wants you to do. When he tells you to get out of your comfort zone and tell others about him, silently sitting in your saved seat in the sanctuary (say that six times in swift succession) isn't really a good option. Maybe you'd rather rehearse your story a little longer. Perhaps you're not terribly sure you will be well received. You question whether you're qualified to go, or you assume that your neighbors will hear the good news from someone else.

But just maybe Jesus is telling you that it's time to quit hanging out with the preacher and the church folks and actually start rubbing shoulders with some lost people.

Come to think of it, he actually put it this way: "It is not the healthy who need a doctor, but the sick" (Matt. 9:12).

pursuing today

Reflect on this: Could Jesus be challenging you to move from theory to practice as you pursue him? What is keeping you from "returning home and telling others what God has done for you"? Obey him. Introduce (or reintroduce) yourself to the people who live right around you. And then begin to tell them how Jesus has changed you.

DAY 23

go

> Then Jesus came to them and said, "All authority in heaven and on earth has been given to me. Therefore go and make disciples of all nations, baptizing them in the name of the Father and of the Son and of the Holy Spirit, and teaching them to obey everything I have commanded you. And surely I am with you always, to the very end of the age."
>
> —*Matthew 28:18–20*

One hot summer day in 1956, a young family—father, mother, and eight-year-old son—was enjoying a lazy Sunday afternoon at home in St. Joseph, Illinois. Two men knocked on the front door. One was named Orville Hubbard. Orville used to work in the oil fields. He had minimal education and was a very normal, ordinary guy. His friend was named Dick Wolf, and he had met this young family when the wives were in the hospital giving birth at the same time several years before. Orville and Dick asked if they could come in; they wanted to talk for a few minutes about something really important to them. There was not much else to do, so the husband invited them in.

He sat on the couch with his wife as Orville and Dick

began to present the gospel. They talked about what it meant to have a relationship with Jesus Christ. The couple sat and listened. Their eight-year-old son, playing with his trucks on the floor, was listening, too, and hanging on every word. That day changed everything for that family. The next week, the mom and dad—along with their young son—gave their lives to Christ and were baptized. Two ordinary men responded to Jesus' missional command to "go and make disciples," and Jesus pointed them to this family's house.

The "Great Commission" of Jesus is not simply a wonderful suggestion. It's not a strategic idea or a devotional illustration. It is an authoritative command. God sent Jesus to make a way for all of mankind to be rescued. And now Jesus sends us to spread that good news. *Go*. Sure, it would be more comfortable to stay. It would be easier to invite them to come to us. *Go*. Yes, the fear factor would be lower, the expenses cheaper, the risk of rejection slighter. But Jesus commands us: *Go*.

Of course, he doesn't send us alone. He promises to be right beside us every step of the way. And he doesn't place the entire burden of responsibility on our shoulders: We plant seeds, we water; but God gives the growth. Still, our part in the mission is to go. Tell. Make disciples, teaching them to obey Jesus too.

I'm sure that Orville and Dick could have found other things to do that day. My guess is they were pretty nervous when they knocked on that door. But two men obeyed Jesus' command to join in his mission. By the way, the couple who answered the door that day I call Grandpa and Grandma. That little eight-year-old boy playing on the floor is now my dad. I think it's fair to say that without Orville and Dick's willingness to *go*, I might not be a Christian today.

pursuing today

Take some time to trace your own spiritual family tree. Do some homework; make some calls. This might take some time, but it could be very rewarding. Thank God for obedient parents, coworkers, or friends. Now consider this: Who is Jesus calling you to go and tell? Eternity is at stake. Commit to respond in obedience today.

DAY 24

not so alarming

"Today, if you hear his voice, do not harden your hearts."
—*Hebrews 3:15, quoting Psalm 95:7–8*

On a recent flight, I found myself thumbing through the shopping catalog I found in the seat-back pocket in front of me. You know, the one tucked between the airline magazine and the barf bag. The one full of products that you never knew existed and are now convinced you couldn't possibly live without.

And on this particular flight, I discovered what my incomplete life had been missing: the gentle progression gradual wake-up alarm clock. It had obvious appeal, promising to wake me up gently and gradually using the beautiful sounds of the Tibetan singing bowl while emitting a slow, warming glow into the sleeper's chambers, reminiscent of a serene mountain sunrise. (Don't lie—you're intrigued now too.)

But then it occurred to me: Doesn't this kind of defeat the purpose of an alarm clock? Isn't the alarm *supposed* to be rousing, not calming? Shouldn't it command our attention and require a response?

Many of us want the gentle progression version of pursuing Jesus. We're okay with pursuing his plan for our lives as long as he allows us to adjust to it gradually. As long as it isn't too shocking or uncomfortable. As long as he doesn't demand an immediate response or drastic action. We'll say yes to Jesus, but only after we've hit the snooze button a few times.

But the gentler the alarm, the harder it can be for us to hear. The longer we put it off, the harder it is for us to respond. Eventually we may find that we just sleep right through it. What Jesus asks is often challenging and uncomfortable. It will interrupt our routine and call us to action. Why not jump up and go ahead and get moving?

Fortunately, he loves each one of us enough to keep sounding the alarm even when we grow deaf to it. But why wait for something more shocking to happen before we respond with obedience? The time is now and the day is today. Say yes to whatever he's asking you to do.

pursuing today

What has Jesus asked you to do that you have been putting off? What mission has he called you to that you are reluctant to accept? What change have you been hesitant to make? Check into that mission trip; sign up for that Bible study; walk across the street and meet your new neighbor; pick up the phone and volunteer at the shelter. Today.

DAY 25

thirty-eight-year wait

> Now there is in Jerusalem near the Sheep Gate a pool, which in Aramaic is called Bethesda and which is surrounded by five covered colonnades. Here a great number of disabled people used to lie—the blind, the lame, the paralyzed. One who was there had been an invalid for thirty-eight years. When Jesus saw him lying there and learned that he had been in this condition for a long time, he asked him, "Do you want to get well?"
>
> —*John 5:2–6*

Jesus' question seems unnecessary. Here's a crippled man lying next to a pool of healing and Jesus asks if he wants to get well. You almost expect the guy to respond with a sarcastic, "Well, sir, I'm not here working on my tan!" Why did Jesus bother to ask?

I am beginning to understand. I've discovered there are a lot of people who like to hang around the pool, but they don't really want to be healed. They like to come to church, but they don't really want to change. They don't mind listening to a message, but they like things the way they are and don't want to give up their "poolside" lifestyle. They say, "I can't get into the pool," when what they really mean is "I won't."

Maybe you're afraid of change. ("We'd really have to downsize.") Maybe you've had thirty-eight years to get used to a certain way of living. ("It's not a *great* marriage, but it's a marriage.") Maybe you're surrounded by dozens of unhealed others and have lost sight of what liberty in Christ could mean. ("Well, at least I'm a better father than he is.")

Maybe you're too ashamed of the condition of your heart. Maybe you still think you can make it on your own. Maybe you doubt that you have much of anything to offer the kingdom. Maybe you think it's just too late for you. You have sensed the call of God to live on purpose—on mission—but for whatever reason, you're hesitant to take action. God is calling you to take the plunge, but you've grown comfortable lounging by the pool.

But Jesus doesn't usually speak in the language of *tomorrow*. Instead, he calls to you *today*. He's not asking, "What if?" He wants you to consider "What now?" Ephesians 5 challenges us, "Be very careful, then, how you live—not as unwise but as wise, making the most of every opportunity, because the days are evil. Therefore do not be foolish, but understand what the Lord's will is" (Eph. 5:15-17).

So today would be a great day to settle the question. As a follower of Jesus, are you ready to follow *wherever*, go *whenever*, and do *whatever* he is asking of you?

pursuing today

What have you given up on or gotten used to? Think of a time (or times) when you clearly sensed that God wanted you to make a change or take some action. Write down what you are hearing. Share your intentions with a friend who will hold you accountable. And prayerfully resolve to "jump in" today.

a prayer for the pursuit

God, chasing you has been more fun than I thought it would be, because you have allowed me to find you. Really, what has become clear is that you are the one who pursued me and found me. It sure is boring and tedious to look for someone you never find, but it is so rewarding to find someone you've searched for high and low.

As I pursue you, daily life becomes more fun as you reveal truth about yourself. I know, though, it will also be dangerous. Finding the God of creation and discovering his plan is an amazing adventure. God, I want to know your mission for me; I want to discern your will for me. I have already received and run after my first assignment: to accept your love and love Jesus in return. My first pursuit is loving you with all my heart. My second is to truly love people.

Thank you for being faithful to me when I have been stubborn and passive. I can see your heart in your Word and in your work and in your world. Your pursuit of me is what makes me chase you. And finding you makes all the chasing more than worth it. Thank you for pursuing me first. I am coming back toward you all the time.

Amen.